The Vision of Hume

David Appelbaum gained his Ph.D. from Harvard University and his M.A. from Exeter College, Oxford. He has studied and taught philosophy for more than thirty years and is currently a professor of philosophy at State University College, New Paltz, New York. In addition to his contributions to a wide range of periodicals, his publications include the acclaimed *Everyday Spirits*, *Voice, The Stop, Disruption, Real Philosophy*, which he co-authored with Jacob Needleman, and *The Vision of Kant*. He has edited and reviewed widely and is currently editor for *Parabola* magazine.

The Spirit of Philosophy Series

"This series of books offers the core teachings of the world's greatest philosophers, considered for the light their writings throw on the moral and material crises of our time. Repositioned in this way, philosophy and the great philosophers may once again serve humankind's eternal and ever-new need to understand who we are, why we are here, and how we are to live."

Jacob Needleman, PH.D.
Series Editor

In the same series

THE SPIRIT OF PHILOSOPHY SERIES

The Vision of Hume

Introduced and edited by
David Appelbaum

ELEMENT

Rockport, Massachusetts ● Shaftesbury, Dorset
Brisbane, Queensland

Text © David Appelbaum 1996

First published in the U.S.A. in 1996 by
Element Books, Inc.
42 Broadway, Rockport, MA 01966

Published in Great Britain in 1996 by
Element Books Limited,
Shaftesbury, Dorset SP7 8BP

Published in Australia in 1996 by
Element Books Limited
for Jacaranda Wiley Limited
33 Park Road, Milton, Brisbane 4064

Cover design by Max Fairbrother

Designed and typeset by Linda Reed and Joss Nizan

Printed and bound in the U.S.A. by
R.R. Donnelley & Son.

Library of Congress Cataloging in Publication data available
British Library Cataloguing in Publication data available

ISBN 1-85230-850-8

CONTENTS

PART TWO: SELECTIONS FROM HUME'S WRITINGS

PART ONE
General Introduction

 Why We Read Hume

Through an extraordinary oversight, David Hume has been largely neglected as a spiritual giant of the modern Western tradition. This is a result of two different factors. First, a reputation as an iconoclast and agnostic—spread by his enemies during his own lifetime—continues to undercut his stature as a thinker of great originality and insight about inner matters. The novelty of his approach drew reactions that branded him as godless, immoral, and inhumane, much in the same way that a new paradigm of consciousness is offensive to those attached to the old.

Second, the rediscovery of Hume, by historical accident (or irony), was initiated by British academy philosophers who, in search for their own roots, believed they found them in Hume's ideas. Since their approach is analytic and literal-minded, Hume has come to be taught as a prototypical ordinary-language philosopher who stresses common sense as the anodyne to flights of metaphysical fancy. According to their interpretation, Hume's method is negative and debunking, and his aim is to demonstrate that since reality is the way common sense perceives it, ordinary perception offers an infallible standard by which all thinking must be judged.

If, however, we disregard the effects of a received interpretation and lingering reputation, Hume strides forth in a very different spirit. His negations now serve a high purpose; to show what humans of the modern age are capable of, one must see clearly how they are at present. Against this clarity of vision that clears the ground of pretention, Hume can provide tools for beginning a search for new meaning. He is remarkably communicative about the specifics of such a search, and is equally sensitive to the fact that we belong to modernity, and that what once was open to men and women for their self-perfection no longer is. Hume leads us immediately and directly to the alchemy of consciousness. Other philosophers, notably Kant and the German idealists, will pick up where he leaves off. But no other thinker of his time is able to discern and assemble the instruments needed for human transformation. Nor is any able to speak to us as simply with regard to the need to become who we are, but are not yet.

 Hume's Life

David Hume was born on 16 April 1711, seventy years after Descartes' publication of the *Meditations on First Philosophy* (1641), sixty years after Hobbes' *Leviathan* (1651), a generation after Locke's *An Essay Concerning Human Understanding* (1689), and contemporaneous with Leibniz's *Monadology* (1714). In Europe, traditionalism was eroded by wave after wave of new ideas. Experimental science enjoyed its first major successes in the fields of mechanics and chemistry. Music and the visual arts abounded with novelty. As New World riches affected established economies, revolutionary changes in governance, violent or otherwise, were rewriting the political map of Great Britain and the Continent.

Edinburgh, Hume's birthplace, and all of Scotland were in the backwash of this new current. Scotland's economy, largely primitive agriculture, was depressed; the force of industrialization had not yet moved north from England. Life was stagnant, even declining, as centers of population lost tradespeople to the southern centers of industry. Religion provided solace, but it was a religion adapted to the barren, austere countryside of Scotland; a popularized, puritanical Calvinism, darkened and made more grim and threatening, was then in vogue.

Election and reprobation were, according to the doctrines of the faithful, served on humankind by a despotic God, swift to wrath. Coupled with them was a need for "enthusiasm," a devotional attitude affected by those hoping to be among the elect.

Hume grew up on his family's estate, Ninewells, outside Edinburgh, a reticent and introspective young man, preoccupied with his own moral character. He was encouraged by his mother to study law at university, but he soon gave this up and instead pursued his interest in, as he said, "books of reasoning and philosophy, and to poetry and the polite authors." Add to this list natural sciences and history, and we have an idea of the food for thought of an omniverous intellect. Hume left before getting a degree, but he emerged from his university years a different person, extroverted and genial, with an marked aversion to organized religion, from which he never recovered. Whatever the cause of the shift in his outlook, religious hypocrisy—in the guise of highblown metaphysical speculation—became a favorite target of his philosophical barbs.

The French sceptic Pierre Bayle was the focus of an early intellectual interest. In 1734, Hume began a three-year stay in France, principally at La Flèche, where Descartes had been schooled over a century earlier. There, at the age of twenty-seven, Hume completed *A Treatise of Human Nature*, subtitled *Being an Attempt to Introduce the Experimental Method of Reasoning into Moral Subjects*. Published in 1739–40, the *Treatise*, as Hume himself said, "fell dead-born from the press, without reaching such distinction as even to excite a murmur among the zealots." Although Hume had expected a more supportive reception to his "revolutionary" work, discouragement did not interfere with his rewriting each of the three books of the *Treatise*. Book I, in its new form, appeared as *Philosophical Essays Concerning Human Understanding* in 1748, revised as *An Enquiry Concerning Human Understanding* in 1758. Book II, in reduced form, became the *Dissertation on the Passions* (1757), while Book III was transformed into *An Enquiry Concerning the Principles of Morals* (1751). The extensive recasting of his ideas in these works met with no warmer reception than had the *Treatise*, and not until very late in his life did he gain the literary success he craved.

Following publication of the *Treatise*, Hume wrote on diverse subjects while working at occupations as varied as tutor, private secretary to General St. Clair (who planned an invasion of Canada), emissary to the courts of Vienna and Turin, and librarian. His *Essays Moral and Political* (1741–42), published anonymously, brought him a first measure of fame. *Political Discourses* (1752) found an appreciative following in France. It was followed by the six-volume *History of England* (1754–62) which made "le bon David" the intellectual darling of France.

In the last decade of his life, Hume became involved in a public dispute with Jean Jacques Rousseau, who harbored groundless fears that Hume was trying to defame him. In the acrimony, Hume's even temper deserted him.

Because of Hume's attitudes toward religious hypocrisy, his reputation was seasoned with bitterness, and he was consistently attacked by the religious right. Many felt his writings to be blasphemous, and Hume himself apparently was prepared to be excommunicated by the General Assembly of the Kirk. He had begun in dialogue form, around 1750, a work that dealt directly with spiritual insincerity and other questions of religion, but he did not want the work to appear during his lifetime. He instructed his friend, the economist, Adam Smith to withhold *Dialogues Concerning Natural Religion* from publication until at least two and a half years after his death. Smith nearly burned the manuscript, and when it finally appeared in 1779, the *Dialogues* had no publisher's name.

Although a controversial figure, Hume, by the end of his life, was popular in the literary world—an achievement he had eagerly sought. But it would be a mean-spirited assessment of Hume to suggest his main drive was fame. As he says at the end of Book I of the *Treatise*, "my only hope is that I may contribute a little to the advancement of knowledge"—a worthy motivation (*Treatise*, I.IV.vii). The lucid awareness and good cheer he manifested while dying from cancer places him in the great philosophical tradition from Socrates and Epicurus to Augustine and Descartes, of performing a meditation on life, not death.

A thinker's philosophical perceptions embody his or her temperament, and Hume's thought is no exception. Adam Smith's appreciation of him paints a portrait of a man who clothed himself in thought:

> His temper . . . seemed to be more happily balanced, if I may be allowed such an expression, than that perhaps of any other man I have ever known. . . . The extreme gentleness of his nature never weakened either the firmness of his mind or the steadiness of his resolutions. His constant pleasantry was the genuine effusion of good-nature and good-humor, tempered with delicacy and modesty, and without even the slightest tincture of malignity, so frequently the disagreeable source of what is called wit in other men. . . . And that gaiety of

temper, so agreeable in society, but which is so often accompanied with frivolous and superficial qualities, was in him certainly attended with the most severe application, the most extensive learning, the greatest depth of thought, and a capacity in every respect the most comprehensive. Upon the whole, I have always considered him, both in his lifetime and since his death, as approaching as nearly to the idea of a perfectly wise and virtuous man, as perhaps the nature of human frailty will permit.

(Letter to William Strahan)

The Way to Knowledge

Observational Awareness and the Humean Revolution

In a letter to his friend Henry Home written in 1739, the year before publication of the first book of the *Treatise*, Hume acknowledges a stunning conviction, that, if understood, "my principles . . . would produce almost a total alteration in philosophy; and you know, revolutions of this kind are not easily brought about." Even now, two hundred and fifty years later, the practice of Hume's revolutionary turn is as difficult as its results are startling. For that turn is toward the subject of philosophy: the philosopher that thinks, "doubts, understands, affirms, denies, wills, refuses, and that also imagines and senses" (Descartes, *Meditations* II.28), who invisibly tints every result with laws of his or her subjectivity. Until such lawful action is taken into account, philosophy will veer toward speculative fantasy or "dogmatic rationalism," where, without an anchor in reality, it will founder on the shoals of conflicting claims and contradictory positions, and eventually destroy itself.

These sobering thoughts make it imperative to include Hume in our intellectual bearing. His primary discovery is of a missing step in philosophical work. Before him, philosophical thought gathered up the results of its investigations in epistemology, metaphysics, ethics, aesthetics, and politics as though that thought itself played no role in arriving at its conclusions. The operations of mind were naively taken as transparently for granted. After Hume, this no longer can be the case. He brings to the fore a form of awareness previously overlooked by an entire philosophical tradition, and utilizes it in his proposed reformulation of the mind's nature and purpose. Of this new awareness, *observational awareness*, he writes, "as the science of man is the only solid foundation for the other sciences, so the only solid foundation we can give to this science itself must be laid on experience and observation" (*Treatise*, Intro.). Philosophy must cultivate an observational awareness of its own processes—in the diverse dimensional activities of intellect—if it wishes to avoid a highblown irrelevancy.

If pursuit of observational awareness is revolutionary, the revolution is a subtle one. The explosion, muted and gradual, is inward. Quite possibly, Hume himself remains unaware of its full significance. The restraint he urges—not to "go beyond experience"—requires a vigilance toward the mind that, seemingly commonplace and learned in the course of things, is, in fact, rare and seldom acquired without long effort. A sense of presence toward inner events (intellectual, emotional, and physical) necessitates a revaluation of thought and values, but not necessarily in a sudden, violent upheaval. Everywhere in Hume, an even-handed, middle-way approach reminds us of the need for gentle persistence, impartial assessment, and openness of attitude toward our work. Observation mandates being exploratory. In Hume's words,

> We must therefore glean up our experiments in this science from a cautious observation of human life, and take them as they appear in the common course of the world, by men's behaviour in company, in affairs, and in their pleasures. Where experiments of this kind are judiciously collected and compared, we may hope to establish on them a science, which will not be inferior in certainty, and will be much superior in utility to any other of human comprehension. (*Treatise*, Intro.)

At the same time, because observational awareness involves an exploration, Hume's proposal is not of a new method. "Method" suggests an approach more fixed and systematic than observation. Hume's reference to science may sound like a call to method, but the term "science" in his day was softer and less rigidly defined. To observe the workings of the mind while it is at work requires art and artistry, a resourceful use of the conditions given, and great flexibility of the attention. Observing the life of the mind is not different from living that life consciously. For Hume, experience is conscious experience. His conviction—that a proper science of conscious experience has the force of revolutionizing the meaning and, hence, the accomplishments, of human existence—is indeed grand.

Scepticism and the Life of Impressions

From an impartial study of his own mind, Hume came up with a series of innovative discoveries far ahead of his time. Chief among these is that of impressions. As consciousness shifted from an open to a more self-contained stance in the Renaissance, the problem of external reality arose. Can we know that the world "out there" is the way we think it to be? Although Descartes and Locke allude to impressions, it is Hume who clearly discerns their force.

Impressions are the unprocessed, unthought, undigested, and unlearned components of mind. As such, they are defined only negatively, in relation to the other mind components, ideas, which are analyzed, classified or interpreted products of thought. Impressions belong to immediacy. They are formless, objectless configurations of energy that affect our perceptual apparatus, both internal and external. By contrast, ideas are mediated by the body of concepts that constitutes the "filter" through which we take in reality. That body contains elements that are personal as well as cultural, inherited as well as acquired. Hume's work parallels a distinction in Vedic thought between *nirvikalpanic* and *visayagatic* perception.

Impressions relate to ideas in two ways, in terms of content and of energy. With content, the impression is to the idea as the original is to the facsimile, while with energy, the idea is the residue or decomposition of the impression. Hume notes that mental processings "may mimic or copy the perceptions of the senses; but they never can entirely reach the force and vivacity of the original sentiment" (*Enquiry*, II.10). In terms of both content and energy, mediated or interpreted experience involves loss—of the unique, mind-stunning power of originality. Inasmuch as our ideas are ciphers of knowledge, human knowledge itself stands under the sign of deprivation. This conclusion, as much as any other, drives Hume toward the scepticism he embraces.

The existential consequences of Hume's research have emerged most clearly in twentieth-century revelations of alienated, despair-ridden experience. Mirroring Hume's own strategy for coping with his philosophical discoveries (see below), they reveal a deep need for impressions. Knowledge alone, lacking the spark of immediacy, starves the human being of the substance of reality that is essential to life. Well-being, which emanates from a state of wholeness, is replaced by mere cognitive functioning, a feature of one part of our being: "The most lively thought is still inferior to the dullest sensation" (*Enquiry*, II.10). The grave results of deprivation of impressions yield a shrunken human potential, a calculative "thinking machine" whose prime concern is the outcome of his or her cognitive ventures. Cut off from a need to be and to explore being, humanity becomes one-dimensional, mental, and without conscience.

Impressions, Hume tells us, include "all our sensations, passions and emotions, as they make their first appearance in the soul" (*Treatise*, I.I.i). They are the *prima materia* capable of transforming the coarser into the finer operations of the attention. Inasmuch as each impression is a whole and of the whole, each could help sustain a higher awareness and a search for meaning. Since each impression has an unbounded, uncircumscribed energy, each can convey a sense of the infinite. Each impression is capable of evoking wonder or awe. Certainly, impressions come into play in Hume's own observational mode of inquiry. To observe the mind at work is basically to experience the sensation of thought. A "science of man" that remains experimental in approach—the fundamental meaning of Hume's empiricism—is rooted in this "lively" impression. Observation, impression, and precognitive experience are the corner-stones of a philosophy that is most often cognitively interpreted.

Hume observes that what commonly takes place is the opposite of refinement, a fall into habit. The primary logic of habit is to copy. An idea is a copy of an impression. An impression is a uniqueness, an utter specificity, a suchness, and an incomparability. It is a copy of nothing, the same as no other. In a subtle form, the habit of copying leads the mind to rely less on impressions and more on their duplicates, ideas. Under sway of habit, the mind retreats from an open stance toward reality and relies more on its conceptual version of what is real. This retreat is marked by a continual contraction of the attention, beginning with its expansion with impressions and ending with an ever tightening focus on thoughts. The human brow becomes furrowed in thought like Rodin's sculpture *The Thinker*.

Is there a reverse current to this downward spiral? If there is, it would recoup the loss of attention and reclaim freedom from habit of mind. Although he only hints at it, Hume suggests that through observational awareness and the science of man, the cognitive machinery can be diagrammed and charted. A thorough knowledge of the machine's limits, its love of assumption and its use of groundless and illusory ideas, can alone provide the means to well-grounded thought in service of what is higher. Not every person is temperamentally equipped to carry out the arduous inquiry. Hume himself bows out after completing only the destructive phase of exposing reason's delusions. The spirit of exploration—empiricist philosophy itself—encourages an extension of his work into regions beyond his purview.

Ideas and Reality

While impressions are energy forms emanating from an unknown source, their degenerate copies, ideas, are the mind's own product designed to delimit and bound experience, developed for the purpose of information and control. While an impression might imbue a mind with surpassing awe, the mental processing that yields the label "tree" informs it of identity, use, relation, possibility, and value. In a utilitarian universe, the idea is an invaluable aid to perception and action. The wonder-struck savage, to coin an example for Hume, could never know what to do with the shimmering play of his impressions, unless he invented the idea of a tree. Ideas answer to the human urge to do and to control. They are first instruments of a human consciousness that instruments itself against reality.

Hume's interest in the mechanics of thought construction extends to the generation of complete thoughts. Leaving aside "relations between ideas," in which one thought follows another by definition (like 2+2=4 or "A carnivore eats meat"), all other thoughts, or "matters of fact," exhibit a certain sequencing that suggests another mechanical principle at work. Hume calls it association, the means by which ideas "introduce each other with a certain degree of method and regularity" (*Enquiry*, III.14).

Association is the name of an involuntary connection of one thought to the next by which reasoning on different levels ordinarily proceeds. Association moves the mind in a dreamlike flow of thought (the so-called stream of consciousness) as well as in deliberative or deductive reasoning. Associative thought relies on three principles: resemblance, contiguity, and cause and effect. That all ordinary uses of reason are associative means that the mind, so conceived, is a clockwork that operates independently of conscious purpose. An intention can recall a certain combination of ideas (memory) or make up a different one (imagination), but in either case, a conscious act merely initiates a mechanical program.

That ordinary thought is calculative and mechanical could lead a thinker to deep pessimism or total scepticism. Hume's embrace of a more moderate position suggests that he grasps the possibility of another, higher, nonautomatic aspect of mind. In an offhand moment, he alludes to an altogether different approach. Nature, he says,

> cures me of this philosophical melancholy and delirium, either by relaxing this bent of mind or by some avocation and lively impressions of my senses which obliterate all these chimeras. (*Treatise*, I.IV.vii)

A receptivity to impressions and their rejuvenative quality opens to a new, nonmechanical mind. Through observation, itself an action of a conscious mind, one can hope with reason to participate in an intelligence aware of higher realities. The nature of another mind, moreover, is to be explored in the gaps, opened by observation, in the everyday, mechanical mind. Hume would acknowledge himself to be at the very beginning of such a project.

Since ideas are products of the human mind, their correspondence with reality is an important issue. Does anything "out there" resemble what we call a "tree," or is our idea mere fantasy (or "fancy")? Hume's reply is subtle and worrisome. Although we can assert that an impression is the cause of an idea, its copy, we can say nothing about the cause of an impression or what in reality it corresponds to. In an argument that will rouse Immanuel Kant from his "dogmatic slumber," Hume points out that causation itself is a mental construct that links thoughts to thoughts. It is incapable of linking thoughts to reality. As to what evokes impressions, "these ultimate springs and principles are totally shut up from human curiosity and enquiry" (*Enquiry*, IV.19). Like John Locke before him, who called the real cause "a something I know not what," Hume places knowledge of reality beyond the reach of the mechanical mind.

With the mind caged by its own constructions and lacking access to the world, we need a criterion to distinguish valid ideas from false ones. Otherwise, thought becomes a gibberish instead of an expression of truth. Philosophy also turns into a pouring "from the empty to the void" since we lack means of rejecting a metaphysical profundity on the basis of noncorrespondence with reality. Rather than succumb to nihilism, Hume proposes that since impressions bear the signature of reality (if only we could read it), they should be used to sort fanciful, contradictory, highblown, or empty-headed ideas from sound ones. Tracing an idea backward to its source in impressional experience pronounces the soundness of that idea. In philosophical work in particular, Hume says,

> When we entertain, therefore, any suspicion that a philosophical term is employed without any meaning or idea (as is but too frequent), we need but enquire, *from what impression is that supposed idea derived?* And if it be impossible to assign any, this will serve to confirm our suspicion. (*Enquiry*, II.13)

The backward or regressive search directs attention away from mental automatism and toward a conscious appreciation of reality. To behold the limits of knowledge is to awaken a humility which alone can undercut the arrogant projects of intellect.

Hume's proposal, the rule of empirical meaning, relieves thought of its isolation. By bringing awareness to the mind's associative wanderings and turning toward precognitive immediacy, the rule initiates a tacit inquiry after life, force, and energy. The shimmering content of impressions, born of a momentary conjunction of the mind and a real influx, raises the standard of intelligence that thought is invited to follow. Hume's work consists wholly in articulating and exemplifying the rule of empirical meaning. It is fair to say that his research is an open file, welcoming the additions of contributors, coworkers, and critics. To approach Hume is to follow the thread of his concern through the labyrinth of the human mind toward an unknown center.

Innate Ideas and the Roots of the Mind

Is all that we know learned from experience or is there knowledge that predates anything the world can teach? The question, its source in antiquity, is answered by Plato and much of Greek thought by reference to the Forms. The Form of, for example, beauty or justice, exists independently of human time and informs us in particular instances of this beautiful person or that just society. The existence of pre-experiential knowledge or of universals is a position held also by medieval thinkers like Plotinus, Boethius, Augustine, and Duns Scotus. As a unitary vision of the cosmos is gradually replaced by a more fragmentary, atomistic one in Renaissance ideas, the notion of pre-experiential knowledge grows more suspect. That ideas could proceed from a higher level of intelligence is rejected in favor of all ideas arising on the same level.

John Locke, in *An Essay Concerning Human*

Understanding (1689), first argues explicitly against the notion of innate ideas. The mind, for him, is a *tabula rasa* or blank slate at birth. All knowledge must be learned; there is no unlearned knowledge, original to the human being. Primarily because "there are none to which all mankind gives a universal assent," Locke denies the existence of innate ideas. Hume is more complicated on the subject. In one regard, he generally accepts Locke's position, though he equates it with the rule of empirical meaning: all ideas come from corresponding impressions. In another regard, he allows that "understanding by innate, what is original or copied from no precedent perception, then may we assert that all our impressions are innate and our ideas not innate" (*Enquiry*, II.13n). That impressions are original is an astounding discovery. It means not only that they provide material for copies but also that they stand at the *origin* of knowledge. Impressions are the original stuff of the mind. Since the mind has impressions before it learns ideas of any particular, it is originally informed by impressional, precognitive experience. Its original information comes by way of participation in an unthought consciousness. At the same time, the approach to original knowledge and a consciousness mindful of origin is through impressions.

The view that each impression is of the origin startles Kant and goads him into writing the *Critique of Pure Reason*. For Hume actually places the mind's center of gravity outside its intellect, that is, its calculative, analytic function. Kant will concede the presence of knowledge independent of all experience, but such pre-experiential knowledge must be assigned to cognition. What for Kant is innate is a conceptual framework, a grid, through which impressional experience must pass.

That a primacy Hume accords to immediacy is immediately lost to Kant and succeeding generations reminds us of the evanescent nature of Hume's discovery. An impression is a momentary energy configuration. It is of the moment. To form or formulate its content is to distort its identity and to obscure the awareness needed to register it. One can say that we, at best, are always on the verge of losing Hume's discovery.

The Illusion of Causation

The child asks, "What is the cause of rainbows?" "What makes water soft?" "Why is grass green?" Answering, we resort to the idea of cause. The idea of cause is so central to the human mind that it is difficult to imagine thought without it. Its explanatory power is unrivalled, its influence on world views without parallel. System after system of philosophical reflection has relied on the idea of cause to elaborate meaning and value. Thus, Hume's discovery of the mechanical mind and the role of cause and effect delivers a stunning blow to thought's arsenal. If causation is but another mind construct, its use guarantees no revelation of reality. To say that grass is green because of its absorption of light may or may not say anything about the nature of the world. It is to speak of the nature of ideas. Whether the one corresponds to the other, we can never know. This is the meaning of Hume's scepticism.

The self-enclosed nature of the mechanical mind is clear to Hume. By habit, thought comes to rely on what it learns by habit, or "custom" as Hume calls it. The shortcut or line of least resistance—"a propensity to renew the same act or operation, without being impelled by any reasoning or process of the understanding"—

replaces a conscious effort to know (*Enquiry*, IV.28). The downward gravitational tendency, he feels, is a fact with no further explanation: "we can push our enquiries no farther, or pretend to give the cause of this cause" (*Enquiry*, IV.28). No matter why we lapse from reasoning or a "process of the understanding," it is paramount to acknowledge that an effortless operation of thought has come to replace a higher, more conscious function. When Hume declares, "All inferences from experience, therefore, are effects of custom, not of reasoning," he points not to the inevitability of involuntary thought but to its prevalence (*Enquiry*, IV.28). To acknowledge the causal or karmic nature of mind is a first step toward opening to the world.

Custom, "the great guide of human life," answers to a need for control. Without it, Hume remarks, "We should never know how to adjust means to ends, or to employ our natural powers in the production of any effect" (*Enquiry*, IV.29). It is both guarantor and fruit of instrumental value. Regarding the need to produce, accomplish, and undertake, Hume tells us

> it is not probable, that it could be trusted to the falla-cious deductions of our reason, which is slow in its operations; appears not in any degree during the first years of infancy; and at best is, in every age and period of human life, extremely liable to error and mistake. (*Enquiry*, V.37)

Although the mechanical mind allows great human accomplishment, its cost is also great. The principle "makes us expect, for the future, a similar train of events with those which have appeared in the past" (*Enquiry*, IV.29). Expectation blocks out novelty. It desensitizes the receptive layer through which impressions pass. It leaves us starved and anemic. On the extent to which we are able to reverse the trend and take in real food for thought, Hume remains noncommittal. That reversal involves a sacrifice of control and a return to a submissive relation to experience. It is precisely the "total alteration in philosophy" Hume mentions in his letter to Henry Home. To accept the revolutionary turn depends on factors external to its merits.

The whole fabric of mind-constructed knowledge is woven by custom. Its causal pattern too is no exception. When event A (lightning) precedes and is always followed by event B (thunder), we are apt to claim that lightning is the cause of thunder or that thunder is the effect of lightning. A "constant conjunction" of events triggers the idea of causation to explain their connection. Hume, however, warns that in fact the connection is between thoughts in the mind, not events in the world. What is absent is "knowledge of the secret power, by which the one object produces the other" (*Enquiry*, IV.28). That gate is barred as long as ordinary thought maintains its impure, unconscious relation to immediacy. To search for a new relation is tantamount to seeking out hidden knowledge.

The world as known is presented through the weavings of custom. Although in itself the world is unknown, we have a sense of reality and by means of that sense ordinarily distinguish between what is there and what is imagined to be there—or as Hume puts it, between "belief" and fiction. Has the sense of reality a conscious sense or is it also a product of custom? The first would ensure that we are already in possession of a discernment of the real. The second would indicate that discernment is yet to be acquired, if possible. For Hume, the case is clearly with the second. A sense of reality, or belief, "is nothing but a more vivid, lively, forcible, firm, steady conception of an object than what the imagination also is ever able to attain" (*Enquiry*, V.32). The enhanced vividness has no relation to what is really out there. It supplies no proof in the way that evidence presents itself to consciousness. That the sense serves in a purely mechanical way means that it is given, not earned. It has the double-edged value of the given. Because we believe we know what is real, the sense obviates a struggle for conscious discernment of reality until its role is brought to light. Hume confesses that to further clarify it is "a very difficult, if not an impossible task" (*Enquiry*, V.32). Yet an awareness of the automaticity that confers reality on thought and perception deepens the inquiry into understanding.

The Illusion of Personal Identity

Is there a real "I," an individuality, that stands out from the gamut of experience I call my own and confers upon it an identity of the person I am? Or is this "I" another fiction that belief plants in the mind but that has no bearing to reality? Hume is a modern to the extent that he raises for our time the question of the self's identity. His novel discussion of the self treads between a nihilism (no self) and an eternalism (an unchanging self), and sets a tone for present day discussions of the subject.

My everyday conception of myself is based on the idea that I am the one who acts in or is acted upon by events of my life. I like, I want, I think, I write, or alternatively, I am recognized or I am devastated. Several assumptions support the ordinary idea. The subject is assumed to exist from the moment of birth (or some such moment) to that of death. Its existence is independent of knowledge of its existence; I exist whether or not I am conscious of the fact. The existence, moreover, cannot be taken away; it is inalienable.

Belief in a constancy or permanence of the self is reinforced by other factors. Use of the first-person singular pronoun "I" in reference to experiences of my life makes it sound as though one and the same being lives from beginning to end. Grammar seems to confirm ontology. I also have one and the same name throughout my life. I respond to being called, sign letters, and introduce myself by that name. Finally, my body undergoes changes so gradually that it seems identical, lending credence to my belief in an enduring identity of self.

Our naive belief, Hume reminds us, must come from an impression if the idea is to have meaning. The idea of a unitary and abiding self, therefore, must derive from a single, unique impression that, as Hume says, "must continue invariably the same through the whole course of our lives" (*Treatise*, I.IV.vi). Such an idea is absent for two reasons. First, the idea of a changeless subject can arise only from a invariable impression of the same. But since the face of change characterizes all aspects of our lives, to seek an impression immune to change is a wildgoose chase. It is to deny the dynamics of life itself.

Second and more radically, no single impression of self exists but rather a collection whose constituents bear a resemblance to one another. A particular pain and a particular desire both seem mine without being derived from one and the same "substance." Combined with the fact that experience occurs in a constant body environment, we mistake resemblance for an abiding and unique impression. All there is, in fact, is a series of specific experiences or scenes with no lead character starring throughout. As Hume relates,

> When I enter most intimately into what I call *myself*,
> I always stumble on some particular perception or
> other, of heat or cold, light or shade, love or hatred,
> pain or pleasure. I never can catch *myself* at any
> time without a perception, and never can observe
> any thing but the perception. (*Treatise*, I.IV.vi)

Hume isolates the fundamental confusion underlying the
question of a real "I." That we believe the self exists and
that it does not is the contradiction Hume wishes to
expose. We can mark the distinction between an uninterrupted sameness of experience (numerical identity) and a
succession of related experiences (qualitative identity or
resemblance). The first is a property of an authentic self,
while the second merely reinforces our unsubstantiated
belief in the self. Until we become sensitive to the difference and explore the groundlessness of ordinary belief,
we are unable to examine an experience of numerical
identity. The momentum of habit, which Hume deplores,
goes against us.

> Our propensity to this mistake is so great from the
> resemblance above-mentioned, that we fall into it
> before we are aware; and though we incessantly
> correct ourselves by reflection, and return to a more
> accurate method of thinking, yet we cannot long
> sustain our philosophy or take off this bias from the
> imagination. (*Treatise*, I.IV.vi)

Apparently, it takes an arduous training to notice the dis-
continuity of perception to which Hume alludes. Each
experience usually seems compacted on the next without
a break. Nature seems to erase the gap in the way that
the visual field erases the retinal blind spot. Yet it is only

by an awareness of a break that we notice a lack of continuity, and so slough off our habitual belief in an abiding being we call our self.

The import of Hume's discussion of personal identity shows that what we call the self is a makeshift, a convenience of reference, or a word lacking a real counterpart. But does this mean that no self exists? The psychophysical or psychosocial self, one might agree, is a thought construct. If we are deluded about its existence, that delusion is not an ordinary one. The risk in all matters where custom, not awareness, is in charge is that the "revolution" of discovery will be costly. That we habitually confound resemblance with identity and refuse consciousness of the fact suggests much is at stake in a belief that a self exists. What is that? Until the emptiness of achievement is experienced, belief in the self is advanced by each urge to undertake and to do. Only when esteem of the self collapses is the reality of our nothingness felt.

Hume's research on the self drives him to pessimism for two reasons. First, the fragility of awareness enables us to distinguish a contingent identity from a necessary one only momentarily. For Hume, only a steady awareness can bring conviction in the self's unreality. With constancy lacking, a conviction about reality is constantly imperilled. Second, that ordinary self-love masks an absence of self does not necessarily mean that we are "designed" to be without a self. What we are needs to be understood in relation to what we might become. To become a being with a self requires a long, careful study of the conditions of inner change as well as an embodiment of the conclusions.

Because Hume is unaware of the full implications of

observational awareness, he is unable to avail himself of
the treasures it holds and he falls into a despair remedied
only by distracting himself:

> I dine, I play a game of backgammon, I converse,
> and am merry with my friends; and when after three
> or four hours' amusement, I would return to these
> speculations, they appear so cold and strained and
> ridiculous that I cannot find in my heart to enter into
> them any farther. (*Treatise*, I.IV.vii)

The data of observational awareness that gradually reveal
an absent self also lay down a path to the presence of
self. A further extension of Hume's experiential method
confirms the mysterious transaction that occurs in the
face of absence. An impression of nonexistence is, as
Hume seems to have overlooked, an impression. It,
moreover, has the singular power to awaken us to the
possibility of existence. That impression calls forth a will-
ingness to search for the means of becoming oneself.
The dawn of the will indicates a great shift in the meaning of observational awareness.

To persist in an effort of observation initiates a
change of vision—in what is seen, in what sees, and in
the seeing itself. Observing becomes an embodying and
participating. Hume's scepticism operates out of a
detachment. As soon as the mind re-engages itself in the
process of beholding, a growth of being takes place.

Scepticism and Beyond

The sceptic is one who practices an attitude or has a
propensity toward doubt. By scepticism, Hume intends a
philosophical position more precise and demanding than
that of the everyday sceptic. It results from a clear vision

of a discrepancy between what we claim to be capable of and what we actually are. The achievements of thought and deed are not so much products of will and intention as involuntary and unconscious by-products. Hume repeatedly observes that while the source of knowledge lies over the horizon, we observe custom at work. Habit, a mechanical operation, does what we customarily believe originates with ourselves. We are mere instruments of these "secret powers."

Nothing runs more deeply in Hume than the contrast between strength of habit and weakness of consciousness.

> Our reason must be considered as a kind of cause of which truth is the natural effect; but such a one as by the irruption of other causes, and by the inconstancy of our mental powers, may frequently be prevented. (*Treatise*, I.IV.i)

Although reason is capable of glimpses of reality, it is underdeveloped and embryonic. Habit or second nature is full-blown and operational. If awareness suffers by the contrast, still the idea is not to replace one by the other. That would attempt the impossible since a mechanical side has its rightful place in our functioning.

> Nature, by an absolute and uncontrollable necessity, has determined us to judge as well as to breathe and feel; nor can we any more forbear viewing certain objects in a stronger and fuller light, upon account of their customary connection with a present impression, than we can hinder ourselves from thinking as long as we are awake, or seeing the surrounding bodies when we turn our eyes towards them in broad sunshine. (*Treatise*, I.IV.i)

To cultivate a sceptical outlook is at once to deflate reason's exaggerated claims and to support its fledgling strength through awareness. The first means a critical attitude toward metaphysics, the second, a greater interest in the bounds of knowledge.

Hume's example of a metaphysical claim is that of the permanent and uninterrupted existence of things external to us. Perception is met with the ever changing flux of one impression, cut off by a second, a third, and so on. An involuntary construction of an abiding object is effected by cognition in the blink of an eye. By habit, the thought construct replaces the shimmering impression. Hume may lament the human dilemma that cognitive knowledge alone does not alter the situation.

> Nature is obstinate and will not quit the field, however strongly attacked by reason; and at the same time reason is so clear in the point that there is no possiblity of disguising her. (*Treatise*, I.IV.i)

He may also perceive how delicate the attention presently is, and where the battleline is drawn:

> As long as our attention is bent upon the subject, the philosophical and studied principle may prevail; but the moment we relax our thoughts, nature will display herself and draw us back to our former opinion. (*Treatise*, I.IV.i)

Nonetheless, if the quality of attentiveness is to be increased, only a steady look at its present condition can serve as a starting point. In that, scepticism provides what is only a realistic look at our present condition.

It may seem to follow from a cultivation of scepticism that philosophy is an anguished and dreaded occupation that goes against natural tendencies, and that only "through gritted teeth" is the philosopher moved to engagement. Hume sounds this mood when he writes, "Where I strive against my inclination, I shall have a good reason of my resistance" (*Treatise*, I.IV.vii). To speak in this vein places too heavy an emphasis on the negative side of philosophy. As humans, we move along the line between a complete captivation by, and a striving for freedom from and toward, life. In this oscillation, Hume recognizes the *need* to do philosophy. To answer the need brings enjoyment, hope, and renewal of motivation. Promise of positive results rather than release from despair feeds an impulse to do philosophy. "I feel," Hume says,

> an ambition to arise in me of contributing to the instruction of mankind. . . . These sentiments spring up naturally in my present disposition; and should I endeavor to banish them by attaching myself to any other business or diversion, I *feel* I should be a loser in point of pleasure; and this is the origin of my philosophy. (*Treatise*, I.IV.vii)

The Moral Sphere

The Illusion of Free Choice

If there is a moral sphere, where thought and deed follow from an ethical principle, it must be based on freedom of choice. Otherwise, external conditions continue to determine the course of action as surely as putting a match to a cannister of gasoline determines an outcome. Freedom, moreover, involves an awareness that alternative actions that engender different sets of consequences are possible. It also requires an ability to embark on an alternative, once selected, and to maintain the choice in the face of difficult circumstances. The freedom of morality is not that of free association but of a rigorous, vigilant consciousness, ever mindful of threats to its will.

Customarily, we humans behave as though we possess free choice. We ascribe existence to a moral sphere in which judgment on the basis of principle affects the outcome of action. Barring the amoralist, knowledge of right and wrong is commonly thought to be a factor in decision making. Discernment of a good *versus* an evil is held to influence behavior in a moral way. We underpin the common point of view with the assumption of voluntary action; we assume that desire is sufficient to impel us to try to attain the object. Thus, when Hume calls into question the fundamental condition necessary for morality—awareness—he initiates a radical revaluation of what we usually hold to be the case in the moral sphere.

Hume's theory of knowledge, we have seen, presents a critical assessment of the power of reason. As we are now, he believes, consciousness consistently defers to habit. The observation that conditioned behavior is the rule, awareness the exception, gives him the prerogative to drive home his rejection of free choice. Without awareness, the realm of voluntary action goes out to the vanishing point. Freedom becomes an illusion, a phantom of the mind, a projection of a dream. Hume states with great certitude, "*first*, that reason alone can never be a motive to any action of the will; and *secondly*, that it can never oppose passion in the direction of the will" (*Treatise*, II.III.iii). The belief that we are free is a habitual form of protection against the realization of our mechanical nature—and the work entailed in coming to possess freedom.

Although he repudiates free choice, Hume does not so much deny as reposition the moral sphere. If freedom is illusory to humanity as it is, there is at least what passes under the name of morality—and Hume will consider it as such. Commonly speaking, morality concerns the relation between motives and voluntary actions, for instance, whether a frank word was said to cause pain (and is blameworthy) or to honestly appraise conduct (praiseworthy), or whether someone was pushed to avoid harm (rightness) or to cause injury (wrongness). To study morality, moreover, requires an investigation of the very same forces that observation has found at work in the mind. Hume notices

> that the conjunction between motives and voluntary actions is as regular and uniform as that between the cause and effect in any part of nature; but also that this regular conjunction has been universally acknowledged among mankind and has never been the subject of dispute, either in philosophy or common life. (*Enquiry*, VIII.59)

Henceforward, morality and epistemology derive from identical principles. In fact, although the former seems like a special application of the latter, it is more likely that Hume's analysis of cause and effect derives from that of motive and action, given his mind-centered approach.

The replacement of an ethics of freedom by an ethics of causation may be a bitter pill to swallow. There is puzzlement in Hume when he confesses

> why all mankind, though they have ever without hesitation acknowledged the doctrine of necessity in their whole practice and reasoning, have yet discovered such a reluctance to acknowledge it in words and have rather shown a propensity in all ages to profess the contrary opinion. (*Enquiry*, VIII.61)

The discrepancy marks the same deep illusion about ourselves: that the will, not external circumstances, is the spring of action. What perpetuates the illusion, moreover, is an unacknowledged (and unremediable) deficiency in our knowledge of causes. The assumption is that causation denotes a real, or in Hume's words, "necessary," connection between events, while the fact is that it is a conceptual tool, a mind construct, for conveniently organizing experience. To overlook the distinction is to suppose "there is a difference between the effects, which result from material force, and those which arise from thought and intelligence" (*Enquiry*, VIII.61). The fact is that on one hand what in reality causes a person to act cannot be known, and on the other a constant conjunction of motive and act can be observed. Philosophy must begin with actuality, not impossibility.

The foregoing argument provides a strong pragmatic reason to accept Hume's repositioned moral sphere. His views on moral psychology provide another when he notices "a great uniformity among the actions of men, in all nations and ages, and that human nature remains still the same, in its principles and operations" (*Enquiry*, VIII.55). One and the same motive—passion or sentiment, in Hume's language—causes the same action because "Mankind are so much the same, in all times and places, that history informs us of nothing new or strange in this particular" (*Enquiry*, VIII.55). Laying aside Hume's blindness to difference, we can say that as for mechanics, so for ethics; universal laws of "constant conjunction" govern human dispositions toward virtuous or vicious acts. The role of a moral philosopher is to lay the laws bare. The role of the statesman or politician is to shape behavior in the light of those laws for the benefit of good government.

The Meaning of Ethics

Just as mechanical laws rather than awareness stand behind moral acts, so too they impel us to moral judgments. Right and wrong, good and bad, and virtue and vice do not express objective qualities of actions or a way of relating to such actions. They rather name a feeling generated by associations caused by an impression of the action. Hume says, "when you pronounce any action or character to be vicious, you mean nothing, but that from the constitution of your nature you have a feeling or sentiment of blame from the contemplation of it" (*Treatise*, III.I.i). Awareness of an impartial principle that governs the conduct of all reasonable beings is no factor. The meaning of an ethical judgment derives solely from a moral feeling, the keynote of moral experience. Morality, as it has been repositioned, is a subjective affair that lacks any objective counterpart. Taking Hume's conclusion in a narrow and negative way, Kant objects strongly enough to write his *Groundwork to a Metaphysics of Morals*.

The moral feeling (or "moral sense") arising through associative means is in its basic make up pleasant or unpleasant. We feel "the impression arising from virtue to be agreeable, and that proceeding from vice to be uneasy." Like the sense of reality ("belief") *vis à vis* the world, so too nature has endowed humanity with an ability to distinguish *in an automatic way* the good from the bad. An electrical transformer mechanically changes magnetic force to its electrical counterpart. Similarly, our moral "transformer" changes an impression of pleasure into a moral judgment. Since the pleasure principle is a nearly infallible device, humankind is guaranteed a consistent and uniform production of moral assessments. Nothing is left to the vagaries of awareness whose untrained nature would result only in indecision.

The analogy between the sense of reality and the moral sense is not perfect. Judgments of fact, unlike moral judgments, can be true or false. Although the former can correspond or fail to correspond to the impression from which they derive, moral judgments have no pictorial value. Since they are intellectual reactions to the force of pleasure, their worth lies in guiding conduct. They are primitive behavior modifiers, themselves susceptible to modifying influences like public opinion, law, and social norms.

One further thought belongs to the relation between the moral senses and the judgments they evoke. Hume notes that "in every system of morality which I have hitherto met with," arguments proceed from premises of a factual nature to a value-laden conclusion. "This change is imperceptible," he says, in moving from an "is" to an "ought," and it is unwarranted by logic. No inferential relation between the two kinds of judgment exists, and to contrive one is to fail to keep differences separate.

What the moral sense "senses" is character or a special valuational quality of a person, specifically, virtuousness or viciousness. "The very essence of virtue, according to this hypothesis, is to produce pleasure, and that of vice to give pain"—though Hume also makes usefulness a second essential aspect of virtue (*Treatise*, II.I.vii). Although the sense is pleasant if an act provokes a feeling of approval, and unpleasant if not, a personal quality, not an action, is the object of judgment. This is because the moral sense is "excited" by sentiments of pride or humility (when toward oneself) or by love or hatred (when toward others). In turn, these feelings, like signatures of character, are prime motivators of the moral sense. They come into play on the dramatic stage of human life "in all ages" like a constant refrain of a chorus. That we invariably take sides in the drama both reflects a lack of impartiality and an imperfect nature, and assures Hume of a perfectly automatic moral response.

As to *what* the moral sense really is, Hume has a reply tucked away in the *Enquiry*. To attempt to define the feeling is to try "to define the feeling of cold or passion of anger to a creature who never had any experience of these sentiments" (*Enquiry*, V.32). To define the sense is no more necessary to philosophy than to define "mass" or "point" is to physics. Inasmuch as the meaning is made known by its function in human life, everyone who reacts approvingly or disapprovingly to a display of character (one's own or another's) possesses meaningful data on the moral sense. Until there is a nonreactive response (one not mediated by conditioned likes or dislikes) to character, these data exhaust the province of morality.

Sympathy

Although Hume, following the tradition of Descartes and Spinoza, examines several feelings at length, he reserves a special role for sympathy. Sympathy, in pre-Renaissance thought, was a cosmological force that bound together unlike beings belonging to different levels of reality. It was a secret power that manifested in the form of correspondences between, for instance, the heliotrope and the sun. Because the heliotrope's, flower constantly follows the path of the sun, a careful observer finds a resemblance (in function, meaning, or force) between the two. To discover the hidden sympathies of things is to understand the purpose of creation. By making the dissimilar similar and drawing opposites together, sympathy cements the whole. It is the unifying force of the cosmos.

Sympathy, for Hume, retains its central and mysterious position in the new empiricist surroundings. Resemblance, one of the three relations between thoughts, is nothing other than sympathetic attraction

elevated to the realm of ideas. Even while being con-
strained by its mental boundaries, resemblance threatens
to explode into a force greater than the intellectual role
Hume assigns it. An example of resemblance is that "a
picture naturally leads our thoughts to the original"
(*Enquiry*, III.14). The concealed power of sympathy is to
move in a direction opposite to habit, from mentally
processed experience back to immediacy. Stale, enervat-
ed thought ascends by way of sympathetic imagination
to be recharged, living impressions. "In sympathy there is
an evident conversion of an idea into an impression"
(*Treatise*, II.I.xi). Sympathy oversees the passage from
subjective interpretation to objectivity and grants escape
from separateness and isolation of the ego.

In human reason, sympathy plays a lead role. When
thinking about others, sympathy provides the basis of a
common understanding among people. Without the force
of sympathy, each person remains behind a wall of reaction, untouched and unaffected by the other's plight.
Because "an idea of a sentiment or passion may by this
means be so enlivened as to become the very sentiment
or passion," we have fresh data by which to understand
the other person (*Treatise*, II.I.xi).

A pessimist would find evidence for an unremitting
egoism in that ordinarily we carry an idea of ourself to all
situations of our lives. If perception and sensitivity are
strongly influenced by an idea of ourself, can we ever
come to a more objective moral assessment of the other
person? In light of sympathy, however, Hume is more
optimistic. Sympathy can "convey the impression or consciousness of our own person to the idea of the sentiments or passions of others, and makes us conceive
them in the strongest and most lively manner" (*Treatise*,
II.I.xi). Sympathy opens us to the basic resemblance of

one person to all others, regardless of ethnic, cultural, or social diversities. Because of the force of sympathy, "the minds of men are mirrors to one another" (*Treatise*, II.II.v). It is the great guide to the moral sphere.

The driving force behind the moral sense is sympathy. That sense is pleasant or useful if we are approving of another's character, unpleasant or unuseful if disapproving. Approbation itself, Hume tells us, "arises from the survey of all those virtues that are useful to society, or to the person possessed of them" (*Treatise*, III.III.vi). But is that force mechanical or does it stem from a more conscious aspect of ourselves? Hume is ambiguous on the question. Sympathy, in its root meaning, is a "feeling together with" another person. It can signify fellow-feeling, a brute but benevolent reaction to others' lives and fortunes. It can also signify a process of presence in which the conscious reception of an impression of another evokes a quality of feeling. Hume's ambiguity reflects the subtle double image of the moral sphere he projects. Morality concerns humanity both as it is (entirely automatic in thought and action) and as it can become (more reasonable and reasoning).

Justice

Justice concerns the fair distribution of goods and services among people. If a pie is to be divided among six people with identical needs and no real differences, the just solution is equal parts. The solution remains just even if one person feels unfairly treated. Since justice is a matter of reason rather than sentiment, it appears to present a difficulty to the moral sense and to Hume's general conception of the moral sphere. Accordingly, he devotes much thought to the question of justice.

Although people act from a disposition to justice, philosophers fail to recognize that justice is an "artificial," not a natural, virtue. Justice is artificial in two senses. First, while natural virtue represents an automatic, unconscious reaction that is part of the original human design, artificial virtue is man-made, a conditioned product of our social environment. A disposition to justice does not exist in a state of nature. It "would never have been dream'd of among rude and savage men" (*Treatise*, III.II.ii). Second, justice is a mixture of several natural virtues, not a specific disposition unto itself. Hume claims "that there is no such passion in human minds, as the love of mankind, merely as such, independent of personal qualities, of services, or of relation to ourself" (*Treatise*, III.II.i). Convention, political climate, and mass culture collaborate to create the ensemble that is called justice. When "nature provides a remedy in the judgment and understanding, for what is irregular and incommodious in the affections," the result wins our approval and is termed just and virtuous (*Treatise*, III.II.ii).

What is the artifice on which justice rests? Locke, before Hume, argues for one such artifice—a social contract—and Hume's contemporary Jean Jacques Rousseau further elaborates the scheme. A social contract is a tacit or explicit agreement of persons arrived at through a process of deliberation as to the right means of governing a common life. The social contract then constitutes just principles for organizing a state. Bodies of rules or laws stipulate individual and group conduct and subsequently determine morally acceptable and unacceptable action. While the approach is attractive, Hume eschews it because of its emphasis on reason and consciousness over the mechanized reaction of sentiment. For him, usefulness alone automatically propels human interaction along the lines of simple conventions and agreements. His favorite example is that of two men at the oars of a boat. To reach their destination requires them to be in agreement on the task at hand. Woven loosely together, different agreements and conventions make up the fabric of a common life. It is from a sense of the utility that the sentiment of justice arises,

> when men, from their early education in society, have become sensible of the infinite advantages that result from it, and have besides acquired a new affection to company and conversation. . . . (*Treatise*, III.II.ii)

Hume's views on politics follow from his conception of justice. While conventions like government, laws, promises, and division of labor are just and justified in terms of their usefulness, private property is the primary concern. Goods, privately owed, are the material counterparts to thoughts and perceptions, privately experienced. An empiricist approach is committed to the first by virtue of its commitment to the second. The basic entitlement of each person to the validity of his or her private experience is translated into the fundamental convention that spawns all of society. As Hume puts it, "I observe that it will be for my interest to leave another in the possession of his goods, *provided* he will act in the same manner with regard to me" (*Treatise*, III.II.ii). Sympathy then allows the founding of the state since "when this common sense of interest is mutually express'd and is known to both, it produces a suitable resolution and behaviour" (*Treatise*, III.II.ii).

Privacy and sympathy join together to form and conserve a cooperative living venture that is society, in which relations among members are very much like the associative relations binding together ordinary thoughts. Such relations are external, contingent (no "necessary connection!"), and subject to the flux of personal interest and affection. Moved, not by understanding but by involuntary forces, people interact in the fashion of billiard balls. It is clear that justice has as little to do with a conscious perception of social need as ordinary self-interest does with awareness. Hume's vision of a mechanical force that regulates human behavior should not, however, be confused with a socially repressive regime that must (like Hobbes's view) govern an inborn nastiness toward life. Humans are by nature a mix of selfishness and generosity, which, in an environment of scarcity, creates the need for convention and a just disposition.

The Sphere of Religion

The "Religious" Impulse

Hume's critical attitude toward religious phenomena is conditioned by his scepticism toward the metaphysical. Any attempt to delineate a field of experience beyond the physical realm is bound to commit excesses, mystify thought, and blur the line between the understandable and the incomprehensible. At the same time, Hume recognized what Kant would call the "rapture of the sublime." The human mind is repeatedly drawn toward thinking about matters beyond its body of data, both current and future. Like a demented researcher who constructs theories in a bankruptcy of information, and dreams, fantasizes and imagines realities he or she cannot access. Hume's grand mission of the *Treatise* and the *Enquiry* is to establish a clear sense of limits. His procedure is to observe the mind's own operation in order to discern proper from improper function. To let the mind operate within such limits yields valid knowledge. To let the mind wander outside this narrow precinct gives rise to phantom ideas like God, freedom and miracles.

Are such limits fixed and immutable, or is the mind capable of a refinement in its operation? Hume is unaware of a vacillation in his approach to a "cautious observation of human life." On one hand, observation appears to be done by a detached onlooker whose act has no effect on that life. On the other, observation is from within the life itself, a participation whose vision has a profound, if subtle, action on what is seen. Hume's strong emphasis on the first (and disregard of its alternative) apparently leads him to favor a hard line on the mind's limits. The second option implies a more flexible stance in which observational consciousness itself provides an access to an ever expanding horizon of thought. That Hume is so disingenuous as to believe his discovery ineffective in this regard is itself a sceptical conclusion, not warranted by the facts.

One need not read too deeply in Hume to uncover a dual attitude toward the realm of the religious. The duality is characterized on one side by an embrace of the individual search for great knowledge and on the other by a dismissal of the precepts of all organized, institutionalized, or, as he says, "natural" religions. In one breath, Hume heaps praises on true religion, which is "nothing but a species of philosophy" (*Essays*, Green & Grose, vol. ii, 120). In the next, he is ready to declaim religion's ignoble persuasiveness.

> What a noble privilege is it of human reason to attain the knowledge of the supreme Being; and from the visible works of nature be enabled to infer so sublime a principle as its supreme Creator. But turn the reverse of the medal. Survey most nations and most ages. Examine the religious principles which have in fact prevailed in the world. You will

scarcely be persuaded they are anything but sick men's dreams. . . . (*Essays*, G & G, vol ii, 362)

Since religious ideals are products of delirium, they restrain an inborn receptivity to impressions of life. They distort material that alone aids a search for meaning. Hume adds that "an abstract, invisible object like that which *natural* religion alone presents to us cannot long actuate the mind or be of any moment in life" (*Essays*, G & G, vol. i. 220). Stale, worn, out-of-date traditional forms bog perception down in the past, rendering it closed to the present occasion. Such forms beget superstition and fanaticism.

Adherence to forms of religion, moreover, drives away an inquiry into meaning. The place of the search

is now supplied by the modern religion which inspects our whole conduct and prescribes a universal rule to our actions, to our words, to our very thoughts and inclinations; a rule so much the more austere as it is guarded by infinite, though distant, rewards and punishments; and no infraction of it can ever be concealed or disguised. (*Essays* G & G, vol. ii, 303–4)

The rise of dogma that attends the triumph of natural religion is not, however, as pernicious as the manipulation of sentiment. Worship demands a show of belief that tends to encourage hypocrisy: "Many religious exercises are entered into with seeming fervor, where the heart, at the time, feels cold and languid: a habit of dissimulation is by degrees contracted" (*Dialogues*, p. 222). Such a tendency leaves a person cut off from untampered feelings that could indicate the sacred character of life.

Commentaries on Hume tend to stress his critical

attitude and often equate it with a repudiation of religious experience. Hume, however, is more concerned with habit and litany than with heart. "*To know God . . . is to worship him.* All other worship is indeed absurd, superstitious, and even impious," he declares in the *Dialogues* (226). "True religion" serves precisely the function of immunizing the mind against dogma, supersitition, fanaticism, and impiety. That it coincides with the openness of inquiry entitles him to make the otherwise outrageous statement that

> the only persons entitled to (God's) *compassion* and *indulgence* would be the philosophical sceptics, a sect almost equally rare, who, from a natural diffidence of their own capacity, suspend or endeavour to suspend all judgment with regard to such sublime and such extraordinary subjects. (*Dialogues*, 227)

Finally, in a spirit that prefigures Kant's wish to limit reason to leave room for faith, Hume wants to limit religion to leave room for morality. In this spirit, he asserts:

> All the philosophy, therefore, in the world, and all the religion, which is nothing but a species of philosophy, will never be able to carry us beyond the usual course of experience, or give us measures of conduct and behaviour different from those which are furnished by reflections on common life. (*Enquiry*, XI.99)

The fine impressions of religious experience relate to an inner life, a life on a level different from everyday life. These relate to being rather than doing. Accordingly, they dictate no course of action, positive or negative. They are not commandments in an ordinary sense, but principles of our unconditional aspect that emanate subtle influences over the entire social and personal spheres. Since they are not objectifiable, to speak of them is to fall into pretense and excess.

Furthermore, morality itself suffices to regulate and orient ordinary life toward the finer. Moral thinking, not religious revelation, supports this life. In looking at humanity,

> we see a creature whose thoughts are not limited by any narrow bounds, either of place or time; . . . a creature who traces causes and effects to a great length and intricacy, extracts general principles from particular appearances, improves upon his discoveries, corrects his mistakes, and makes his very errors profitable. (*Essays*, G & G, vol. i, 152)

On God's Design

The *Dialogues* provide an extended examination of one traditional argument for God's existence: that from design. In form, the argument from design is not a teleological argument that claims that an examination of the worth, value, or end of the cosmos requires absolutely a divine being for its existence. It is instead an argument from analogy, anthropomorphic in character, that compares products of human creation with the universe and concludes with the necessity of God as prime creator. A corollary is that an ordering intelligence in personal experience provides a model for that intelligence at work behind all creation.

Hume makes his particular approach to the argument of design in a philosophical climate that rejects atheism. By atheism, eighteenth-century thought had in mind the notion that particles of energy, randomly or lawfully interacting, were responsible for the ordered universe. This ancient view, atomism, can be traced back to the pre-Socratic thinkers such as Leucippus and Democritus. Closer to Hume, his predecessor, Francis Bacon, writes his own repudiation of atheism:

> it is a thousand times more credible, that four mutable elements, and one immutable fifth essence, duly and eternally placed, need no God, than that an army of infinite small portions, or seeds unplaced, should have produced this order and beauty without a divine marshal. (*Essays*, XVI. "Of Atheism")

"Out of nothing comes nothing." Since Plato's time, nothing short of a miracle was thought necessary to bring so empty a beginning into fruitful existence. The unintelligibility of cosmic creation that arises from the lower, without the intention of a higher, conscious source is precisely the position Hume arms himself against.

It is incorrect, however, that Hume allies himself with atomism. His approach is more subtle. He first reminds us of his discovery in the *Treatise*, repeated in the *Enquiry*, that though we move from effect back to cause, back to the cause's cause, ultimate or "original" causes are beyond our knowledge. We are entitled to make reference to the impression that causes our idea of something. The source of the impression, however, is and must remain mysterious to our mind. Although opening ourselves to a participation in that source is possible, being, not knowledge, results.

Life (or "organization," as Hume calls it) is also essentially mysterious. Causal knowledge of it is strictly limited and is unable to inform us of the vital springs of life. We say that life is always accompanied by intelligence, or in the case of human beings, consciousness.

That intelligence may provoke wonder and awe, but, in its nature, it is "nothing but a wonderful and unintelligible instinct in our souls" (*Treatise*, I.III.xvi) whose "essence is incomprehensible" (*Dialogues*, 178). The inner source of knowledge is as far removed from being known as the eye is from being seen.

To draw an analogy between life, intelligence, and instinct is merely to delimit a common thread, which is that of order. All three phenomena are alike in requiring an ordering principle. With all three, the principle stands beyond knowledge. If the necessity of God's existence is likened to the way human intelligence supplies order in the human world, Hume's response is indirect. Rather than to repudiate, his interest is to point out the ambiguous, indefinite nature of the conclusion. The argument appears to say much more than it actually does. Like a great wave that washes over the beach and leaves everything just as it was, so too analogy establishes nothing not known beforehand.

Hume's argument is in essence a negative one. It is not an argument for atheism but for a suspension of belief, both theistic and atheistic. It does not question God's existence, but mistaken arguments for it—arguments that breed idolatry and superstition.

Miracles

Although section X of the *Enquiry* is entitled "Of Miracles," its main focus is not the miraculous but the alleged source of miracles, God. Hume warms to the subject because it drives home points on belief, testimony, and evidence to further curb a tendency toward religious speculation. Superstition, idolatry, and fanaticism— an uncritical credulity—are again targets of the inquiry.

Examples of miracles—marvellous healings, vision, apparitions, and prophecies—were as rife in Hume's day as in our own. In fact, both times share a spiritual climate hungry for revelation and epiphanic vision as traditional wisdom goes into hiding. Both are attracted to preposterous, absurd, unbelievable, incredible accounts of supernatural events—if only to settle a gnawing unreason of the age. It is for the sake of an open-ended search that Hume reins in the human love of miracles.

Hume states that a miracle "is a violation of the laws of nature," an event that occurs outside "the common course of nature" (*Enquiry*, X.76). The evidence of impressions establishes a lawfulness of experience that constitutes nature. A constant conjunction of event A with event B provides sure demonstration of their causal relation, even though we must remain ignorant of a real connection. Since miracles run counter to a lawful frame of experience, no experimental proof exists. Hume, however, makes an even stronger case. To claim a miracle has happened amounts to its own disproof. As he puts it,

> no testimony is sufficient to establish a miracle, unless the testimony be of such a kind that its falsehood would be more miraculous, than the fact, which it endeavours to establish. (*Enquiry*, X.77)

If there is a report of someone dead who came back to life, Hume asks "whether it be more probable that this person should either deceive or be deceived, or that the fact, which he relates, should really have happened" (*Enquiry*, X.77). To decide, Hume ironically suggests, weigh each alternative and reject the greater "miracle."

The real object of Hume's venom is not obvious until he notes that inasmuch as miracles arise within a "system of religion," their hope is to establish the existence of the deity who wills them. Such a being, for instance, as described in the Old Testament, is capable of interfering in world events at will and transgressing against the natural course of law. But even if there are miracles, they themselves give no grounds for a God to whom they can be ascribed. The argument echoes Hume's proceedings against design.

The Dialogues

Much of the substance of the *Dialogues* has already been covered. Hume's investigation of design as a basis of Divine Existence is the sceptical thread running through his restraint of metaphysics. A concern for supporting a fledgling observational awareness makes it paramount to dull the attraction of easy revelations and imagined disclosures. The full flower of argument is his way of returning to rough ground, the struggle to maintain an honest and sincere search for truth.

In the *Dialogues*, the narrator, Pamphilus, reports on the views of three protagonists: "the accurate philosophical turn of Cleanthes," "the careless scepticism of Philo," and "the rigid orthodoxy of Demea." Although Hume's own position is dialectically woven by all three, Philo most closely represents what Hume takes to be the case. Cleanthes' and Demea's philosophical limitations are repeatedly shown by the force of Philo's attacks, but never so as to lessen the dramatic impact of the encounter.

The main tenets of Hume's argument can be reconstructed from various passages spoken by Philo:

(1) It looks promising when one attempts to derive the author's existence from the design of life ("generation").

> Judging by our limited and imperfect experience, generation has some privileges above reason: For we see every day the latter arise from the former, never the former from the latter. (179)

(2) The promise evaporates when we see the sleight of hand involved in the reasoning.

> In all instances which we have ever seen, ideas are copied from real objects, and are ectypal, not archetypal, to express myself in learned terms: You reverse this order and give thought the precedence. In all instances which we have ever seen, thought has no influence upon matter except where that matter is so conjoined with it as to have an equal reciprocal influence upon it. (181)

(3) Even if the teleological premises of design are granted, no way exists to derive principles that affect the moral sphere.

> But there is no view of human life or of the condition of mankind, from which, without the greatest violence, we can infer the moral attributes or learn that infinite benevolence, conjoined with infinite power and infinite wisdom, which we must discover by the eyes of faith alone. (201–2)

(4) Thus, the argument is in the position of failing to establish what it seeks to establish—the moral agency of God.

> As the works of nature have a much greater analogy to the effects of *our* art and contrivance, than to those of *our* benevolence and justice, we have reason to infer that the natural attributes of the Deity have a greater resemblance to those of man, than his moral have to human virtues. (219)

(5) The argument's conclusion is too weak to accomplish its aim. The conclusion is that natural religion

> resolves itself into one simple, though somewhat ambiguous, at least undefined proposition, *that the cause or causes of order in the universe probably bear some remote analogy to human intelligence.* (227)

(6) The argument, in its frivolous and inexact use of reason, makes a mockery of a sincere search for divine being.

> Notwithstanding the freedom of my conversation, and my love of singular arguments, no one . . . pays more profound adoration to the divine Being as he discovers himself to reason, in the inexplicable contrivance and artifice of nature. A purpose, an intention, or design strikes everywhere the most careless, the most stupid thinker; and no man can be so hardened in absurd systems, as at all times to reject it. (214)

Conclusion

Hume's argument concerning faith, belief, and testimony extends his defense of reason. Human awareness, in its frail, embryonic condition, needs the protection of clear thinking in order not to be impaled on the stakes of suggestibility. In our hypnotic state, we are too willing to give over a search for meaning to any cause that speaks with conviction and confidence. Only patient exercise of understanding yields a point of view on which we can rely—and even then, neither permanently nor for very long. To question, which Hume asks us to do, requires suspension of easy belief, and equally easy disbelief. It is to accept a life of uncertainty, unsettledness, and irresolution. It is to bear in mind that triumphs are small in the face of the cosmic conundrum that calls us to behold it. "The whole is a riddle," Hume writes,

> an enigma, an inexplicable mystery. Doubt, uncertainty, suspense of judgment appear the only result of our most accurate scrutiny concerning this subject. But such is the frailty of human reason, and such the irresistible contagion of opinion that even this deliberate doubt could scarcely be upheld did we not enlarge our view, and opposing one species of superstition to another, set them quarrelling,

> while we ourselves, during their fury and con-
> tention, happily make our escape into the calm,
> though obscure, regions of philosophy. (*Natural
> History of Religion*, 64)

The advent of observational consciousness is a subtle
event. Its "smallness" might tempt one to dismiss it,
which is the signature of our usual attitude. Yet to
embrace and study it reveals its immense significance. Its
reflectiveness indicates a separation from the stream of
ordinary consciousness. The novelty of the shift is like
that of a balloon filling with helium: one more puff and
the effects of gravity become neutralized.

Hume's discovery of observational consciousness
and the mechanical nature of thought are pregnant with
such novelty. Both are ideas to be read, not by the literal
mind, but by the knowing heart. Made one's own, they
disclose the path of a search. The gradual, step-by-step
itinerary is necessary when the lamp one carries sheds
light barely farther than one's body. Hume's great hope-
fulness is that this sphere suffices, and that as one takes
another step, the darkness recedes by just the corresponding amount.

PART TWO
Selections from Hume's Writings

A Treatise of Human Nature

ed. L. A. Selby-Bigge.
Oxford: Clarendon Press, 1888.

(pp. 251–56)

BOOK I

Of personal identity

THERE are some philosophers, who imagine we are every moment intimately conscious of what we call our SELF; that we feel its existence and its continuance in existence; and are certain, beyond the evidence of a demonstration, both of its perfect identity and simplicity. The strongest sensation, the most violent passion, say they, instead of distracting us from this view, only fix it the more intensely, and make us consider their influence on *self* either by their pain or pleasure. To attempt a farther proof of this were to weaken its evidence; since no proof can be deriv'd from any fact, of which we are so intimately conscious; nor is there any thing, of which we can be certain, if we doubt of this.

Unluckily all these positive assertions are contrary to that very experience, which is pleaded for them, nor have we any idea of *self*, after the manner it is here explain'd. For from what impression could this idea be deriv'd? This question 'tis impossible to answer without a manifest contradiction and absurdity; and yet 'tis a question, which must necessarily be answer'd, if we wou'd have the idea of self pass for clear and intelligible. It must be some one impression, that gives rise to every real idea. But self or person is not any one impression, but that to which our several impressions and ideas are suppos'd to have a reference. If any impression gives rise to the idea of self, that impression must continue invariably the same, thro' the whole course of our lives; since self is suppos'd to exist after that manner. But there is no impression constant and invariable. Pain and pleasure, grief and joy, passions and sensations succeed each other, and never all exist at the same time. It cannot, therefore, be from any of these impressions, or from any other, that the idea of self is deriv'd; and consequently there is no such idea.

But farther, what must become of all our particular perceptions upon this hypothesis? All these are different, and distinguishable, and separable from each other, and may be separately consider'd, and may exist separately, and have no need of any thing to support their existence. After what manner, therefore, do they belong to self; and how are they connected with it? For my part, when I enter most intimately into what I call *myself*, I always stumble on some particular perception or other, of heat or cold, light or shade, love or hatred, pain or pleasure. I never can catch *myself* at any time without a perception, and never can observe any thing but the perception. When my perceptions are remov'd for any time, as by sound sleep, so long am I insensible of *myself*, and may truly be said not to exist. And were all my perceptions remov'd by death, and cou'd I neither think, nor feel, nor see, nor love, nor hate after the dissolution of my body, I shou'd be entirely annihilated, nor do I conceive what is farther requisite to make me a perfect non-entity. If any one upon serious and unprejudic'd reflexion, thinks he has a different notion of *himself*, I must confess I can reason no longer with him. All I can allow him is, that he may be in the right as well as I, and that we are essentially different in this particular. He may, perhaps, perceive something simple and continu'd, which he calls *himself*; tho' I am certain there is no such principle in me.

But setting aside some metaphysicians of this kind, I may venture to affirm of the rest of mankind, that they are nothing but a bundle or collection of different perceptions, which succeed each other with an inconceivable rapidity, and are in a perpetual flux and movement. Our eyes cannot turn in their sockets without varying our perceptions. Our thought is still more variable than our sight; and all our other senses and faculties contribute to this change; nor is there any single power of the soul, which remains unalterably the same, perhaps for one moment. The mind is a kind of theatre, where several perceptions successively make their appearance; pass, re-pass, glide away, and mingle in an infinite variety of postures and situations. There is properly no *simplicity* in it at one time, nor *identity* in different, whatever natural propension we may have to imagine that simplicity and identity. The comparison of the theatre must not mislead us. They are the successive perceptions only, that constitute the mind; nor have we the most distant notion of the place, where these scenes are represented, or of the materials, of which it is compos'd.

What then gives us so great a propension to ascribe an identity to these successive perceptions, and to suppose ourselves possest of an invariable and uninterrupted existence thro' the whole course of our lives? In order to answer this question, we must distinguish betwixt personal identity, as it regards our thought or imagination, and as it regards our passions or the concern we take in ourselves. The first is our present subject; and to explain it perfectly we must take the matter pretty deep, and account for that identity, which we attribute to plants and animals; there being a great analogy betwixt it, and the identity of a self or person.

We have a distinct idea of an object, that remains invariable and uninterrupted thro' a suppos'd variation of time; and this idea we call that of *identity* or *sameness*. We have also a distinct idea of several different objects existing in succession, and connected together by a close relation; and this to an accurate view affords as perfect a notion of *diversity*, as if there was no manner of relation among the objects. But tho' these two ideas of identity, and a succession of related objects be in themselves perfectly distinct, and even contrary, yet 'tis certain, that in our common way of thinking they are generally confounded with each other. That action of the imagination, by which we consider the uninterrupted and invariable object, and that by which we reflect on the succession of related objects are almost the same to the feeling, nor is there much more effort of thought requir'd in the latter case than in the former. The relation facilitates the transition of the mind from one object to another, and renders its passage as smooth as if it contemplated one continu'd object. This resemblance is the cause of the confusion and mistake, and makes us substitute the notion of identity, instead of that of related objects. However at one instant we may consider the related succession as variable or interrupted, we are sure the next to ascribe to it a perfect identity, and regard it as invariable and uninterrupted. Our propensity to this mistake is so great from the resemblance above-mention'd, that we fall into it before we are aware; and tho' we incessantly correct ourselves by reflexion, and return to a more accurate method of thinking, yet we cannot long sustain our philosophy, or take off this biass from the imagination. Our last resource is to yield to it, and boldly assert that these different related objects are in effect the same, however interrupted and variable. In order to justify to ourselves this absurdity, we often feign some new and unintelligible principle, that connects the objects together, and prevents their interruption or variation. Thus we feign the continu'd existence of the perceptions of our senses, to remove the interruption; and run into the notion of a *soul*, *self*, and *substance*, to disguise the variation. But we may farther observe, that where we do not give rise to such a fiction, our propension to confound identity with relation is so great, that we are apt to imagine[1] something unknown and mysterious, connecting the parts, beside their relation; and this I take to be the case with regard to the identity we ascribe to plants and vegetables. And even when this does not take place, we still feel a propensity to confound these ideas, tho' we are not able fully to satisfy ourselves in that particular, nor find any thing invariable and uninterrupted to justify our notion of identity.

Thus the controversy concerning identity is not merely a dispute of words. For when we attribute identity, in an improper sense, to variable or interrupted

---

[1] If the reader is desirous to see how a great genius may be influenc'd by these seemingly trivial principles of the imagination, as well as the mere vulgar, let him read my Lord *Shaftsbury* reasonings concerning the uniting principle of the universe, and the identity of plants and animals. See his *Moralists* or *Philosophical rhapsody*.

objects, our mistake is not confin'd to the expression, but is commonly attended with a fiction, either of something invariable and uninterrupted, or of something mysterious and inexplicable, or at least with a propensity to such fictions. What will suffice to prove this hypothesis to the satisfaction of every fair enquirer, is to shew from daily experience and observation, that the objects, which are variable or interrupted, and yet are suppos'd to continue the same, are such only as consist of a succession of parts, connected together by resemblance, contiguity, or causation. For as such a succession answers evidently to our notion of diversity, it can only be by mistake we ascribe to it an identity; and as the relation of parts, which leads us into this mistake, is really nothing but a quality, which produces an association of ideas, and an easy transition of the imagination from one to another, it can only be from the resemblance, which this act of the mind bears to that, by which we contemplate one continu'd object, that the error arises. Our chief business, then, must be to prove, that all objects, to which we ascribe identity, without observing their invariableness and uninterruptedness, are such as consist of a succession of related objects.

In order to do this, suppose any mass of matter, of which the parts are contiguous and connected, to be plac'd before us; 'tis plain we must attribute a perfect identity to this mass, provided all the parts continue uninterruptedly and invariably the same, whatever motion or change of place we may observe either in the whole or in any of the parts. But supposing some very *small* or *inconsiderable* part to be added to the mass, or subtracted from it; tho' this absolutely destroys the identity of the whole, strictly speaking; yet as we seldom think so accurately, we scruple not to pronounce a mass of matter the same, where we find so trivial an alteration. The passage of the thought from the object before the change to the object after it, is so smooth and easy, that we scarce perceive the transition, and are apt to imagine, that 'tis nothing but a continu'd survey of the same object.

(pp. 261–62)

As memory alone acquaints us with the continuance and extent of this succession of perceptions, 'tis to be consider'd, upon that account chiefly, as the source of personal identity. Had we no memory, we never shou'd have any notion of causation, nor consequently of that chain of causes and effects, which constitute our self or person. But having once acquir'd this notion of causation from the memory, we can extend the same chain of causes, and consequently the identity of our persons beyond our memory, and can comprehend times, and circumstances, and actions, which we have entirely forgot, but suppose in general to have existed. For how few of our past actions are there, of which we have any memory? Who can tell me, for instance, what were his thoughts and actions on the first of *January* 1715, the 11th of *March* 1719, and the 3d of *August* 1733? Or will he affirm, because he has entirely forgot the incidents of these days, that the present self is not the same person with the self of that time; and by that means overturn all the most establish'd notions of personal identity? In this view, therefore, memory does not so much *produce* as *discover* personal identity, by shewing us the relation of cause and effect among our different perceptions. 'Twill be incumbent on those, who affirm that memory produces entirely our personal identity, to give a reason why we can thus extend our identity beyond our memory.

The whole of this doctrine leads us to a conclusion, which is of great importance in the present affair, *viz.* that all the nice and subtile questions concerning personal identity can never possibly be decided, and are to be regarded rather as grammatical than as philosophical difficulties. Identity depends on the relations of ideas; and these relations produce identity, by means of that easy transition they occasion. But as the relations, and the easiness of the transition may diminish by insensible degrees, we have no just standard, by which we can decide any dispute concerning the time, when they acquire or lose a title to the name of identity. All the disputes concerning the identity of connected objects are merely verbal, except so far as the relation of parts gives rise to some fiction or imaginary principle of union, as we have already observ'd.

(pp. 316–21)

BOOK II

Of the love of fame

No quality of human nature is more remarkable, both in itself and in its consequences, than that propensity we have to sympathize with others, and to receive by communication their inclinations and sentiments, however different from, or even contrary to our own. This is not only conspicuous in children, who implicitly embrace every opinion propos'd to them; but also in men of the greatest judgment and understanding, who find it very difficult to follow their own reason or inclination, in opposition to that of their friends and daily companions.

To this principle we ought to ascribe the great uniformity we may observe in the humours and turn of thinking of those of the same nation; and 'tis much more probable, that this resemblance arises from sympathy, than from any influence of the soil and climate, which, tho' they continue invariably the same, are not able to preserve the character of a nation the same for a century together. A good-natur'd man finds himself in an instant of the same humour with his company; and even the proudest and most surly take a tincture from their countrymen and acquaintance. A chearful countenance infuses a sensible complacency and serenity into my mind; as an angry or sorrowful one throws a sudden damp upon me. Hatred, resentment, esteem, love, courage, mirth and melancholy; all these passions I feel more from communication than from my own natural temper and disposition. So remarkable a phænomenon merits our attention, and must be trac'd up to its first principles.

When any affection is infus'd by sympathy, it is at first known only by its effects, and by those external signs in the countenance and conversation, which convey an idea of it. This idea is presently converted into an impression, and acquires such a degree of force and vivacity, as to become the very passion itself, and produce an equal emotion, as any original affection. However instantaneous this change of the idea into an impression may be, it proceeds from certain views and reflections, which will not escape the strict scrutiny of a philosopher, tho' they may the person himself, who makes them.

'Tis evident, that the idea, or rather impression of ourselves is always intimately present with us, and that our consciousness gives us so lively a conception of our own person, that 'tis not possible to imagine, that any thing can in this particular go beyond it. Whatever object, therefore, is related to ourselves must be conceived with a like vivacity of conception, according to the foregoing principles; and tho' this relation shou'd not be so strong as that of causation, it must still have a considerable influence. Resemblance and contiguity are relations not to be neglected; especially when by an inference from cause and effect, and by the observation of external signs, we are inform'd of the real existence of the object, which is resembling or contiguous.

Now 'tis obvious, that nature has preserv'd a great resemblance among all human creatures, and that we never remark any passion or principle in others, of which, in some degree or other, we may not find a parallel in ourselves. The case is the same with the fabric of the mind, as with that of the body. However the parts may differ in shape or size, their structure and composition are in general the same. There is a very remarkable resemblance, which preserves itself amidst all their variety; and this resemblance must very much contribute to make us enter into the sentiments of others, and embrace them with facility and pleasure. Accordingly we find, that where, beside the general resemblance of our natures, there is any peculiar similarity in our manners, or character, or country, or language, it facilitates the sympathy. The stronger the relation is betwixt ourselves and any object, the more easily does the imagination make the transition, and convey to the related idea the vivacity of conception, with which we always form the idea of our own person.

Nor is resemblance the only relation, which has this effect, but receives new force from other relations, that may accompany it. The sentiments of others have little influence, when far remov'd from us, and require the relation of contiguity, to make them communicate themselves entirely. The relations of blood, being a species of causation, may sometimes contribute to the same effect; as also acquaintance, which operates in the same manner with education and custom; as we shall see more fully afterwards. All these relations, when united together, convey the impression or consciousness of our own person to the idea of the sentiments or passions of others, and makes us conceive them in the strongest and most lively manner.

It has been remark'd in the beginning of this treatise, that all ideas are borrow'd from impressions, and that these two kinds of perceptions differ only in the degrees of force and vivacity, with which they strike upon the soul. The component parts of ideas and impressions are precisely alike. The manner and order of their appearance may be the same. The different degrees of their force and vivacity are, therefore, the only particulars, that distinguish them: And as this difference may be remov'd, in some measure, by a relation betwixt the impressions and ideas, 'tis no wonder an idea of a sentiment or passion, may by this means be so inliven'd as to become the very sentiment or passion. The lively idea of any object always approaches its impression; and 'tis certain we may feel sickness and pain from the mere force of imagination, and make a malady real by often thinking of it. But this is most remarkable in the opinions and affections; and 'tis there principally that a lively idea is converted into an impression. Our affections depend more upon ourselves, and the internal operations of the mind, than any other impressions; for which reason they arise more naturally from the imagination, and from every lively idea we form of them. This is the nature and cause of sympathy; and 'tis after this manner we enter so deep into the opinions and affections of others, whenever we discover them.

What is principally remarkable in this whole affair is the strong confirmation these phænomena give to the foregoing system concerning the understanding, and consequently to the present one concerning the passions; since these are analogous to each other. 'Tis indeed evident, that when we sympathize with the passions and sentiments of others, these movements appear at first in *our* mind as mere ideas, and are conceiv'd to belong to another person, as we conceive any other matter of fact. 'Tis also evident, that the ideas of the affections of others are converted into the very impressions they represent, and that the passions arise in conformity to the images we form of them. All this is an object of the plainest experience, and depends not on any hypothesis of philosophy. That science can only be admitted to explain the phænomena; tho' at the same time it must be confest, they are so clear of themselves, that there is but little occasion to employ it. For besides the relation of cause and effect, by which we are convinc'd of the reality of the passion, with which we sympathize; besides this, I say, we must be assisted by the relations of resemblance and contiguity, in order to feel the sympathy in its full perfection. And since these relations can entirely convert an idea into an impression, and convey the vivacity of the latter into the former, so perfectly as to lose nothing of it in the transition, we may easily conceive how the relation of cause and effect alone, may serve to strengthen and inliven an idea. In sympathy there is an evident conversion of an idea into an impression. This conversion arises from the relation of objects to ourself. Our self is always intimately present to us. Let us compare all these circumstances, and we shall find, that sympathy is exactly correspondent to the operations of our under-standing; and even contains something more surprising and extraordinary.

'Tis now time to turn our view from the general con-sideration of sympathy, to its influence on pride and humility, when these passions arise from praise and blame, from reputation and infamy. We may observe, that no person is ever prais'd by another for any quality, which wou'd not, if real, produce, of itself, a pride in the person possest of it. The elogiums either turn upon his power, or riches, or family, or virtue; all of which are subjects of vanity, that we have already explain'd and accounted for. 'Tis certain, then, that if a person consid-er'd himself in the same light, in which he appears to his admirer, he wou'd first receive a separate pleasure, and afterwards a pride or self-satisfaction, according to the hypothesis above explain'd. Now nothing is more natural than for us to embrace the opinions of others in this par-ticular; both from *sympathy*, which renders all their senti-ments intimately present to us; and from *reasoning*, which makes us regard their judgment, as a kind of argu-ment for what they affirm. These two principles of authority and sympathy influence almost all our opinions; but must have a peculiar influence, when we judge of our own worth and character. Such judgments are always attended with passion; and nothing tends more to disturb our understanding, and precipitate us into any opinions, however unreasonable, than their connexion with pas-sion; which diffuses itself over the imagination, and gives an additional force to every related idea. To which we may add, that being conscious of great partiality in our own favour, we are peculiarly pleas'd with any thing, that confirms the good opinion we have of ourselves, and are easily shock'd with whatever opposes it.

(pp. 456–61)

BOOK III

Of virtue and vice in general

It has been observ'd, that nothing is ever present to the mind but its perceptions; and that all the actions of seeing, hearing, judging, loving, hating, and thinking, fall under this denomination. The mind can never exert itself in any action, which we may not comprehend under the term of *perception*; and consequently that term is no less applicable to those judgments, by which we distinguish moral good and evil, than to every other operation of the mind. To approve of one character, to condemn another, are only so many different perceptions.

Now as perceptions resolve themselves into two kinds, viz. *impressions* and *ideas*, this distinction gives rise to a question, with which we shall open up our present enquiry concerning morals, *Whether 'tis by means of our* ideas *or* impressions *we distinguish betwixt vice and virtue, and pronounce an action blameable or praiseworthy?* This will immediately cut off all loose discourses and declamations, and reduce us to something precise and exact on the present subject.

Those who affirm that virtue is nothing but a conformity to reason; that there are eternal fitnesses and unfitnesses of things, which are the same to every rational being that considers them; that the immutable measures of right and wrong impose an obligation, not only on human creatures, but also on the Deity himself: All these systems concur in the opinion, that morality, like truth, is discern'd merely by ideas, and by their juxta-position and comparison. In order, therefore, to judge of these systems, we need only consider, whether it be possible, from reason alone, to distinguish betwixt moral good and evil, or whether there must concur some other principles to enable us to make that distinction.

If morality had naturally no influence on human passions and actions, 'twere in vain to take such pains to inculcate it; and nothing wou'd be more fruitless than that multitude of rules and precepts, with which all moralists abound. Philosophy is commonly divided into *speculative* and *practical*; and as morality is always comprehended under the latter division, 'tis supposed to influence our passions and actions, and to go beyond the calm and indolent judgments of the understanding. And this is confirm'd by common experience, which informs us, that men are often govern'd by their duties, and are deter'd from some actions by the opinion of injustice, and impell'd to others by that of obligation.

Since morals, therefore, have an influence on the actions and affections, it follows, that they cannot be deriv'd from reason; and that because reason alone, as we have already prov'd, can never have any such influence. Morals excite passions, and produce or prevent actions. Reason of itself is utterly impotent in this particular. The rules of morality, therefore, are not conclusions of our reason.

No one, I believe, will deny the justness of this inference; nor is there any other means of evading it, than by denying that principle, on which it is founded. As long as it is allow'd, that reason has no influence on our passions and actions, 'tis in vain to pretend, that morality is discover'd only by a deduction of reason. An active principle can never be founded on an inactive; and if reason be inactive in itself, it must remain so in all its shapes and appearances, whether it exerts itself in natural or moral subjects, whether it considers the powers of external bodies, or the actions of rational beings.

It would be tedious to repeat all the arguments, by which I have prov'd, that reason is perfectly inert, and can never either prevent or produce any action or affection. 'Twill be easy to recollect what has been said upon that subject. I shall only recall on this occasion one of these arguments, which I shall endeavour to render still more conclusive, and more applicable to the present subject.

Reason is the discovery of truth or falsehood. Truth or falsehood consists in an agreement or disagreement either to the *real* relations of ideas, or to *real* existence and matter of fact. Whatever, therefore, is not susceptible of this agreement or disagreement, is incapable of being true or false, and can never be an object of our reason. Now 'tis evident our passions, volitions, and actions, are not susceptible of any such agreement or disagreement; being original facts and realities, compleat in themselves, and implying no reference to other passions, volitions, and actions. 'Tis impossible, therefore, they can be pronounced either true or false, and be either contrary or conformable to reason.

This argument is of double advantage to our present purpose. For it proves *directly*, that actions do not derive their merit from a conformity to reason, nor their blame from a contrariety to it; and it proves the same truth more *indirectly*, by shewing us, that as reason can never immediately prevent or produce any action by contradicting or approving of it, it cannot be the source of moral good and evil, which are found to have that influence. Actions may be laudable or blameable; but they cannot be reasonable or unreasonable: Laudable or blameable, therefore, are not the same with reasonable or unreasonable. The merit and demerit of actions frequently contradict, and sometimes control our natural propensities. But reason has no such influence. Moral distinctions, therefore, are not the offspring of reason. Reason is wholly inactive, and can never be the source of so active a principle as conscience, or a sense of morals.

But perhaps it may be said, that tho' no will or action can be immediately contradictory to reason, yet we may find such a contradiction in some of the attendants of the action, that is, in its causes or effects. The action may cause a judgment, or may be *obliquely* caus'd by one, when the judgment concurs with a passion; and by an abusive way of speaking, which philosophy will scarce allow of, the same contrariety may, upon that account, be ascrib'd to the action. How far this truth or falsehood may be the source of morals, 'twill now be proper to consider.

It has been observ'd, that reason, in a strict and philosophical sense, can have an influence on our conduct only after two ways: Either when it excites a passion by informing us of the existence of something which is a proper object of it; or when it discovers the connexion of causes and effects, so as to afford us means of exerting any passion. These are the only kinds of judgment, which can accompany our actions, or can be said to produce them in any manner; and it must be allow'd, that these judgments may often be false and erroneous. A person may be affected with passion, by supposing a pain or pleasure to lie in an object, which has no tendency to produce either of these sensations, or which produces the contrary to what is imagin'd. A person may also take false measures for the attaining his end, and may retard, by his foolish conduct, instead of forwarding the execution of any project. These false judgments may be thought to affect the passions and actions, which are connected with them, and may be said to render them unreasonable, in a figurative and improper way of speaking. But tho' this be acknowledg'd, 'tis easy to observe, that these errors are so far from being the source of all immorality, that they are commonly very innocent, and draw no manner of guilt upon the person who is so unfortunate as to fall into them. They extend not beyond a mistake of *fact*, which moralists have not generally suppos'd criminal, as being perfectly involuntary. I am more to be lamented than blam'd, if I am mistaken with regard to the influence of objects in producing pain or pleasure, or if I know not the proper means of satisfying my desires. No one can ever regard such errors as a defect in my moral character. A fruit, for instance, that is really disagreeable, appears to me at a distance, and thro' mistake I fancy it to be pleasant and delicious. Here is one error. I choose certain means of reaching this fruit, which are not proper for my end. Here is a second error; nor is there any third one, which can ever possibly enter into our reasonings concerning actions. I ask, therefore, if a man, in this situation, and guilty of these two errors, is to be regarded as vicious and criminal, however unavoidable they might have been? Or if it be possible to imagine, that such errors are the sources of all immorality?

And here it may be proper to observe, that if moral distinctions be deriv'd from the truth or falsehood of those judgments, they must take place wherever we form the judgments; nor will there be any difference, whether the question be concerning an apple or a kingdom, or whether the error be avoidable or unavoidable. For as the very essence of morality is suppos'd to consist in an agreement or disagreement to reason, the other circumstances are entirely arbitrary, and can never either bestow on any action the character of virtuous or vicious, or deprive it of that character. To which we may add, that this agreement or disagreement, not admitting of degrees, all virtues and vices wou'd of course be equal.

Shou'd it be pretended, that tho' a mistake of *fact* be not criminal, yet a mistake of *right* often is; and that this may be the source of immorality: I would answer, that 'tis impossible such a mistake can ever be the original source of immorality, since it supposes a real right and wrong; that is, a real distinction in morals, independent of these judgments. A mistake, therefore, of right may become a species of immorality; but 'tis only a secondary one, and is founded on some other, antecedent to it.

As to those judgments which are the *effects* of our actions, and which, when false, give occasion to pronounce the actions contrary to truth and reason; we may observe, that our actions never cause any judgment, either true or false, in ourselves, and that 'tis only on others they have such an influence. 'Tis certain, that an action, on many occasions, may give rise to false conclusions in others; and that a person, who thro' a window sees any lewd behaviour of mine with my neighbour's wife, may be so simple as to imagine she is certainly my own. In this respect my action resembles somewhat a lye or falsehood; only with this difference, which is material, that I perform not the action with any intention of giving rise to a false judgment in another, but merely to satisfy my lust and passion. It causes, however, a mistake and false judgment by accident; and the falsehood of its effects may be ascribed, by some odd figurative way of speaking, to the action itself. But still I can see no pretext of reason for asserting, that the tendency to cause such

an error is the first spring or original source of all
immorality.

(pp. 470–75)

Moral distinctions deriv'd from a moral sense

THUS the course of the argument leads us to conclude,
that since vice and virtue are not discoverable merely by
reason, or the comparison of ideas, it must be by means
of some impression or sentiment they occasion, that we
are able to mark the difference betwixt them. Our deci-
sions concerning moral rectitude and depravity are evidently perceptions; and as all perceptions are either
impressions or ideas, the exclusion of the one is a convincing argument for the other. Morality, therefore, is
more properly felt than judg'd of; tho' this feeling or sentiment is commonly so soft and gentle, that we are apt to
confound it with an idea, according to our common custom of taking all things for the same, which have any
near resemblance to each other.

The next question is, Of what nature are these
impressions, and after what manner do they operate
upon us? Here we cannot remain long in suspense, but
must pronounce the impression arising from virtue, to be
agreeable, and that proceeding from vice to be uneasy.
Every moment's experience must convince us of this.
There is no spectacle so fair and beautiful as a noble and
generous action; nor any which gives us more abhorrence than one that is cruel and treacherous. No enjoyment equals the satisfaction we receive from the
company of those we love and esteem; as the greatest of
all punishments is to be oblig'd to pass our lives with
those we hate or contemn. A very play or romance may

afford us instances of this pleasure, which virtue conveys to us; and pain, which arises from vice.

Now since the distinguishing impressions, by which moral good or evil is known, are nothing but *particular* pains or pleasures; it follows, that in all enquiries concerning these moral distinctions, it will be sufficient to shew the principles, which make us feel a satisfaction or uneasiness from the survey of any character, in order to satisfy us why the character is laudable or blameable. An action, or sentiment, or character is virtuous or vicious; why? because its view causes a pleasure or uneasiness of a particular kind. In giving a reason, therefore, for the pleasure or uneasiness, we sufficiently explain the vice or virtue. To have the sense of virtue, is nothing but to *feel* a satisfaction of a particular kind from the contemplation of a character. The very *feeling* constitutes our praise or admiration. We go no farther; nor do we enquire into the cause of the satisfaction. We do not infer a character to be virtuous, because it pleases: But in feeling that it pleases after such a particular manner, we in effect feel that it is virtous. The case is the same as in our judgments concerning all kinds of beauty, and tastes, and sensations. Our approbation is imply'd in the immediate pleasure they convey to us.

I have objected to the system, which establishes eternal rational measures of right and wrong, that 'tis impossible to shew, in the actions of reasonable creatures, any relations, which are not found in external objects; and therefore, if morality always attended these relations, 'twere possible for inanimate matter to become virtuous or vicious. Now it may, in like manner, be objected to the present system, that if virtue and vice be determin'd by pleasure and pain, these qualities must, in every case, arise from the sensations; and consequently

any object, whether animate or inanimate, rational or
irrational, might become morally good or evil, provided
it can excite a satisfaction or uneasiness. But tho' this
objection seems to be the very same, it has by no means
the same force, in the one case as in the other. For, *first*,
'tis evident, that under the term *pleasure*, we comprehend sensations, which are very different from each
other, and which have only such a distant resemblance,
as is requisite to make them be express'd by the same
abstract term. A good composition of music and a bottle
of good wine equally produce pleasure; and what is
more, their goodness is determin'd merely by the pleasure. But shall we say upon that account, that the wine is
harmonious, or the music of a good flavour? In like manner an inanimate object, and the character or sentiments
of any person may, both of them, give satisfaction; but as
the satisfaction is different, this keeps our sentiments
concerning them from being confounded, and makes us
ascribe virtue to the one, and not to the other. Nor is
every sentiment of pleasure or pain, which arises from
characters and actions, of that *peculiar* kind, which
makes us praise or condemn. The good qualities of an
enemy are hurtful to us; but may still command our
esteem and respect. 'Tis only when a character is considered in general, without reference to our particular interest, that it causes such a feeling or sentiment, as
denominates it morally good or evil. 'Tis true, those sentiments, from interest and morals, are apt to be confounded, and naturally run into one another. It seldom
happens, that we do not think an enemy vicious, and can
distinguish betwixt his opposition to our interest and real
villainy or baseness. But this hinders not, but that the
sentiments are, in themselves, distinct; and a man of
temper and judgment may preserve himself from these

illusions. In like manner, tho' 'tis certain a musical voice is nothing but one that naturally gives a *particular* kind of pleasure; yet 'tis difficult for a man to be sensible, that the voice of an enemy is agreeable, or to allow it to be musical. But a person of a fine ear, who has the command of himself, can separate these feelings, and give praise to what deserves it.

Secondly, we may call to remembrance the preceding system of the passions, in order to remark a still more considerable difference among our pains and pleasures. Pride and humility, love and hatred are excited, when there is any thing presented to us, that both bears a relation to the object of the passion, and produces a separate sensation related to the sensation of the passion. Now virtue and vice are attended with these circumstances. They must necessarily be plac'd either in ourselves or others, and excite either pleasure or uneasiness; and therefore must give rise to one of these four passions; which clearly distinguishes them from the pleasure and pain arising from inanimate objects, that often bear no relation to us: And this is, perhaps, the most considerable effect that virtue and vice have upon the human mind.

It may now be ask'd *in general*, concerning this pain or pleasure, that distinguishes moral good and evil, *From what principles is it derived, and whence does it arise in the human mind?* To this I reply, *first*, that 'tis absurd to imagine, that in every particular instance, these sentiments are produc'd by an *original* quality and *primary* constitution. For as the number of our duties is, in a manner, infinite, 'tis impossible that our original instincts should extend to each of them, and from our very first infancy impress on the human mind all that multitude of precepts, which are contain'd in the compleatest system of ethics. Such a method of proceeding is not

conformable to the usual maxims, by which nature is
conducted, where a few principles produce all that variety we observe in the universe, and every thing is carry'd
on in the easiest and most simple manner. 'Tis necessary,
therefore, to abridge these primary impulses, and find
some more general principles, upon which all our
notions of morals are founded.

But in the *second* place, should it be ask'd, Whether
we ought to search for these principles in *nature*, or
whether we must look for them in some other origin? I
wou'd reply, that our answer to this question depends
upon the definition of the word, Nature, than which
there is none more ambiguous and equivocal. If *nature*
be oppos'd to miracles, not only the distinction betwixt
vice and virtue is natural, but also every event, which has
ever happen'd in the world, *excepting those miracles, on
which our religion is founded*. In saying, then, that the
sentiments of vice and virtue are natural in this sense, we
make no very extraordinary discovery.

But *nature* may also be opposed to rare and unusual; and in this sense of the word, which is the common
one, there may often arise disputes concerning what is
natural or unnatural; and one may in general affirm, that
we are not possess'd of any very precise standard, by
which these disputes can be decided. Frequent and rare
depend upon the number of examples we have observ'd;
and as this number may gradually encrease or diminish,
'twill be impossible to fix any exact boundaries betwixt
them. We may only affirm on this head, that if ever there
was any thing, which cou'd be call'd natural in this
sense, the sentiments of morality certainly may; since
there never was any nation of the world, nor any
single person in any nation, who was utterly depriv'd of
them, and who never, in any instance, shew'd the least

approbation or dislike of manners. These sentiments are so rooted in our constitution and temper, that without entirely confounding the human mind by disease or madness, 'tis impossible to extirpate and destroy them.

But *nature* may also be opposed to artifice, as well as to what is rare and unusual; and in this sense it may be disputed, whether the notions of virtue be natural or not. We readily forget, that the designs, and projects, and views of men are principles as necessary in their operation as heat and cold, moist and dry: But taking them to be free and entirely our own, 'tis usual for us to set them in opposition to the other principles of nature. Shou'd it, therefore, be demanded, whether the sense of virtue be natural or artificial, I am of opinion, that 'tis impossible for me at present to give any precise answer to this question. Perhaps it will appear afterwards, that our sense of some virtues is artificial, and that of others natural. The discussion of this question will be more proper, when we enter upon an exact detail of each particular vice and virtue.

Mean while it may not be amiss to observe from these definitions of *natural* and *unnatural*, that nothing can be more unphilosophical than those systems, which assert, that virtue is the same with what is natural, and vice with what is unnatural. For in the first sense of the word, Nature, as opposed to miracles, both vice and virtue are equally natural; and in the second sense, as oppos'd to what is unusual, perhaps virtue will be found to be the most unnatural. At least it must be own'd, that heroic virtue, being as unusual, is as little natural as the most brutal barbarity. As to the third sense of the word, 'tis certain, that both vice and virtue are equally artificial, and out of nature. For however it may be disputed, whether the notion of a merit or demerit in certain actions be natural or artificial, 'tis evident, that the actions themselves are artificial, and are perform'd with a certain design and intention; otherwise they cou'd never be rank'd under any of these denominations. 'Tis impossible, therefore, that the character of natural and unnatural can ever, in any sense, mark the boundaries of vice and virtue.

(pp. 479–82)

Of justice and injustice

In short, it may be establish'd as an undoubted maxim, *that no action can be virtuous, or morally good, unless there be in human nature some motive to produce it, distinct from the sense of its morality.*

But may not the sense of morality or duty produce an action, without any other motive? I answer, It may: But this is no objection to the present doctrine. When any virtuous motive or principle is common in human nature, a person, who feels his heart devoid of that motive, may hate himself upon that account, and may perform the action without the motive, from a certain sense of duty, in order to acquire by practice, that virtuous principle, or at least, to disguise to himself, as much as possible, his want of it. A man that really feels no gratitude in his temper, is still pleas'd to perform grateful actions, and thinks he has, by that means, fulfill'd his duty. Actions are at first only consider'd as signs of motives: But 'tis usual, in this case, as in all others, to fix our attention on the signs, and neglect, in some measure, the thing signify'd. But tho', on some occasions, a person may perform an action merely out of regard to its moral obligation, yet still this supposes in human nature some distinct principles, which are capable of producing the action, and whose moral beauty renders the action meritorious.

Now to apply all this to the present case; I suppose a person to have lent me a sum of money, on condition that it be restor'd in a few days; and also suppose, that after the expiration of the term agreed on, he demands the sum: I ask, *What reason or motive have I to restore the money?* It will, perhaps, be said, that my regard to justice, and abhorrence of villainy and knavery, are sufficient reasons for me, if I have the least grain of honesty, or sense of duty and obligation. And this answer, no doubt, is just and satisfactory to man in his civiliz'd state, and when train'd up according to a certain discipline and education. But in his rude and more *natural* condition, if you are pleas'd to call such a condition natural, this answer wou'd be rejected as perfectly unintelligible and sophistical. For one in that situation wou'd immediately ask you, *Wherein consists this honesty and justice, which you find in restoring a loan, and abstaining from the property of others?* It does not surely lie in the external action. It must, therefore, be plac'd in the motive, from which the external action is deriv'd. This motive can never be regard to the honesty of the action. For 'tis a plain fallacy to say, that a virtuous motive is requisite to render an action honest, and at the same time that a regard to the honesty is the motive of the action. We can never have a regard to the virtue of an action, unless the action be antecedently virtuous. No action can be virtuous, but so far as it proceeds from a virtuous motive. A virtuous motive, therefore, must precede the regard to the virtue; and 'tis impossible, that the virtuous motive and the regard to the virtue can be the same.

'Tis requisite, then, to find some motive to acts of justice and honesty, distinct from our regard to the honesty; and in this lies the great difficulty. For shou'd we say, that a concern for our private interest or reputation is the legitimate motive to all honest actions; it wou'd follow, that wherever that concern ceases, honesty can no longer have place. But 'tis certain, that self-love, when it acts at its liberty, instead of engaging us to honest actions, is the source of all injustice and violence; nor can a man ever correct those vices, without correcting and restraining the *natural* movements of that appetite.

But shou'd it be affirm'd, that the reason or motive of such actions is the *regard to publick interest*, to which nothing is more contrary than examples of injustice and dishonesty; shou'd this be said, I wou'd propose the three following considerations, as worthy of our attention. *First*, public interest is not naturally attach'd to the observation of the rules of justice; but is only connected with it, after an artificial convention for the establishment of these rules, as shall be shewn more at large hereafter. *Secondly*, if we suppose, that the loan was secret, and that it is necessary for the interest of the person, that the money be restor'd in the same manner (as when the lender wou'd conceal his riches) in that case the example ceases, and the public is no longer interested in the actions of the borrower; tho' I suppose there is no moralist, who will affirm, that the duty and obligation ceases. *Thirdly*, experience sufficiently proves, that men, in the ordinary conduct of life, look not so far as the public interest, when they pay their creditors, perform their promises, and abstain from theft, and robbery, and injustice of every kind. That is a motive too remote and too sublime to affect the generality of mankind, and operate with any force in actions so contrary to private interest as are frequently those of justice and common honesty.

In general, it may be affirm'd, that there is no such passion in human minds, as the love of mankind, merely as such, independent of personal qualities, of services, or of relation to ourself. 'Tis true, there is no human, and indeed no sensible, creature, whose happiness or misery does not, in some measure, affect us, when brought near to us, and represented in lively colours: But this proceeds merely from sympathy, and is no proof of such an universal affection to mankind, since this concern extends itself beyond our own species. An affection betwixt the sexes is a passion evidently implanted in human nature; and this passion not only appears in its peculiar symptoms, but also in inflaming every other principle of affection, and raising a stronger love from beauty, wit, kindness, than what wou'd otherwise flow from them. Were there an universal love among all human creatures, it wou'd appear after the same manner. Any degree of a good quality wou'd cause a stronger affection than the same degree of a bad quality wou'd cause hatred; contrary to what we find by experience. Men's tempers are different, and some have a propensity to the tender, and others to the rougher, affections: But in the main, we may affirm, that man in general, or human nature, is nothing but the object both of love and hatred, and requires some other cause, which by a double relation of impressions and ideas, may excite these passions. In vain wou'd we endeavour to elude this hypothesis. There are no phænomena that point out any such kind affection to men, independent of their merit, and every other circumstance. We love company in general; but 'tis as we love any other amusement. An *Englishman* in *Italy* is a friend:

A *Europœan* in *China*; and perhaps a man wou'd be belov'd as such, were we to meet him in the moon. But this proceeds only from the relation to ourselves; which in these cases gathers force by being confined to a few persons.

If public benevolence, therefore, or a regard to the interests of mankind, cannot be the original motive to justice, much less can *private benevolence, or a regard to the interests of the party concern'd*, be this motive. For what if he be my enemy, and has given me just cause to hate him? What if he be a vicious man, and deserves the hatred of all mankind? What if he be a miser, and can make no use of what I wou'd deprive him of? What if he be a profligate debauchee, and wou'd rather receive harm than benefit from large possessions? What if I be in necessity, and have urgent motives to acquire something to my family? In all these cases, the original motive to justice wou'd fail; and consequently the justice itself, and along with it all property, right, and obligation.

(pp. 623–27)

APPENDIX

THERE is nothing I wou'd more willingly lay hold of, than an opportunity of confessing my errors; and shou'd esteem such a return to truth and reason to be more honourable than the most unerring judgment. A man, who is free from mistakes, can pretend to no praises, except from the justness of his understanding: But a man, who corrects his mistakes, shews at once the justness of his understanding, and the candour and ingenuity of his temper. I have not yet been so fortunate as to discover any very considerable mistakes in the reasonings

deliver'd in the preceding volumes, except on one article: But I have found by experience, that some of my
expressions have not been so well chosen, as to guard
against all mistakes in the readers; and 'tis chiefly to remedy this defect, I have subjoin'd the following appendix.

We can never be induc'd to believe any matter of
fact, except where its cause, or its effect, is present to us;
but what the nature is of that belief, which arises from
the article of cause and effect, few have had the curiosity
to ask themselves. In my opinion, this dilemma is
inevitable. Either the belief is some new idea, such as
that of *reality* or *existence*, which we join to the simple
conception of an object, or it is merely a peculiar *feeling*
or *sentiment*. That it is not a new idea, annex'd to the
simple conception, may be evinc'd from these two arguments. *First*, We have no abstract idea of existence, distinguishable and separable from the idea of particular
objects. 'Tis impossible, therefore, that this idea of existence can be annex'd to the idea of any object, or from
the difference betwixt a simple conception and belief.
Secondly, the mind has the command over all its ideas,
and can separate, unite, mix, and vary them as it pleases;
so that if belief consisted merely in a new idea, annex'd
to the conception, it wou'd be in a man's power to
believe what he pleas'd. We may, therefore, conclude,
that belief consists merely in a certain feeling or sentiment; in something that depends not on the will, but
must arise from certain determinate causes and principles, of which we are not masters. When we are convinc'd of any matter of fact, we do nothing but conceive
it, along with a certain feeling, different from what
attends the mere *reveries* of the imagination. And when
we express our incredulity concerning any fact, we
mean, that the arguments for the fact produce not that

feeling. Did not the belief consist in a sentiment different from our mere conception, whatever objects were presented by the wildest imagination, wou'd be on an equal footing with the most establish'd truths founded on history and experience. There is nothing but the feeling, or sentiment, to distinguish the one from the other.

This, therefore, being regarded as an undoubted truth *that belief is nothing but a peculiar feeling, different from the simple conception*, the next question, that naturally occurs, is *what is the nature of this feeling, or sentiment, and whether it be analogous to any other sentiment of the human mind?* This question is important. For if it be not analogous to any other sentiment, we must despair of explaining its causes, and must consider it as an original principle of the human mind. If it be analogous, we may hope to explain its causes from analogy, and trace it up to more general principles. Now that there is a greater firmness and solidity in the conceptions, which are the objects of conviction and assurance, than in the loose and indolent reveries of a castle-builder, every one will readily own. They strike upon us with more force; they are more present to us; the mind has a firmer hold of them, and is more actuated and mov'd by them. It acquiesces in them; and, in a manner, fixes and reposes itself on them. In short, they approach nearer to the impressions, which are immediately present to us; and are therefore analogous to many other operations of the mind.

There is not, in my opinion, any possibility of evading this conclusion, but by asserting, that belief, beside the simple conception, consists in some impression or feeling, distinguishable from the conception. It does not modify the conception, and render it more present and intense: It is only annex'd to it, after the same manner that *will* and *desire* are annex'd to particular conceptions of good and pleasure. But the following considerations will, I hope, be sufficient to remove this hypothesis. *First*, It is directly contrary to experience, and our immediate consciousness. All men have ever allow'd reasoning to be merely an operation of our thoughts or ideas; and however those ideas may be varied to the feeling, there is nothing ever enters into our *conclusions* but ideas, or our fainter conceptions. For instance; I hear at present a person's voice, whom I am acquainted with; and this sound comes from the next room. This impression of my senses immediately conveys my thoughts to the person, along with all the surrounding objects. I paint them out to myself as existent at present, with the same qualities and relations, that I formerly knew them possess'd of. These ideas take faster hold of my mind, than the ideas of an inchanted castle. They are different to the feeling; but there is no distinct or separate impression attending them. 'Tis the same case when I recollect the several incidents of a journey, or the events of any history. Every particular fact is there the object of belief. Its idea is modified differently from the loose reveries of a castle-builder: But no distinct impression attends every distinct idea, or conception of matter of fact. This is the subject of plain experience. If ever this experience can be disputed on any occasion, 'tis when the mind has been agitated with doubts and difficulties; and afterwards, upon taking the object in a new point of view, or being presented with a new argument, fixes and reposes itself in one settled conclusion and belief. In this case there is a feeling distinct and separate from the conception. The passage from doubt and agitation to tranquility and repose, conveys a satisfaction and pleasure to the mind. But take any other case. Suppose I see the legs and thighs of a person in motion, while some interpos'd object conceals the rest of his body. Here 'tis certain, the imagination spreads out the whole figure. I give him a head and shoulders, and breast and neck. These members I conceive and believe him to be possess'd of. Nothing can be more evident, than that this whole operation is perform'd by the thought or imagination alone. The transition is immediate. The ideas presently strike us. Their customary connexion with the present impression, varies them and modifies them in a certain manner, but produces no act of the mind, distinct from this peculiarity of conception. Let any one examine his own mind, and he will evidently find this to be the truth.

Secondly, Whatever may be the case, with regard to this distinct impression, it must be allow'd, that the mind has a firmer hold, or more steady conception of what it takes to be matter of fact, than of fictions. Why then look any farther, or multiply suppositions without necessity?

Thirdly, We can explain the *causes* of the firm conception, but not those of any separate impression. And not only so, but the causes of the firm conception exhaust the whole subject, and nothing is left to produce any other effect. An inference concerning a matter of fact is nothing but the idea of an object, that is frequently conjoin'd, or is associated with a present impression. This is the whole of it. Every part is requisite to explain, from analogy, the more steady conception; and nothing remains capable of producing any distinct impression.

Fourthly, The *effects* of belief, in influencing the passions and imagination, can all be explain'd from the firm conception; and there is no occasion to have recourse to any other principle. These arguments, with many others, enumerated in the foregoing volumes, sufficiently prove, that belief only modifies the idea or conception; and renders it different to the feeling, without producing any distinct impression.

Thus upon a general view of the subject, there appear to be two questions of importance, which we may venture to recommend to the consideration of philosophers, *Whether there be any thing to distinguish belief from the simple conception beside the feeling or sentiment?* And, *Whether this feeling be any thing but a firmer conception, or a faster hold, that we take of the object?*

If, upon impartial enquiry, the same conclusion, that I have form'd, be assented to by philosophers, the next business is to examine the analogy, which there is betwixt belief, and other acts of the mind, and find the cause of the firmness and strength of conception: And this I do not esteem a difficult task. The transition from a present impression, always enlivens and strengthens any idea. When any object is presented, the idea of its usual attendant immediately strikes us, as something real and solid. 'Tis *felt* rather than conceiv'd, and approaches the impression, from which it is deriv'd, in its force and influence. This I have prov'd at large. I cannot add any new arguments; tho' perhaps my reasoning on this whole question, concerning cause and effect, wou'd have been more convincing, had the following passages been inserted in the places, which I have mark'd for them. I have added a few illustrations on other points, where I thought it necessary.

An Enquiry Concerning Human Understanding

ed. Eric Steinberg.
Indianapolis: Hackett, 1977.

(pp. 9–15)

SECTION II

Of the Origin of Ideas

EVERY one will readily allow, that there is a considerable difference between the perceptions of the mind, when a man feels the pain of excessive heat, or the pleasure of moderate warmth, and when he afterwards recalls to his memory this sensation, or anticipates it by his imagination. These faculties may mimic or copy the perceptions of the senses; but they never can entirely reach the force and vivacity of the original sentiment. The utmost we say of them, even when they operate with greatest vigour, is, that they represent their object in so lively a manner, that we could *almost* say we feel or see it: But, except the mind be disordered by disease or madness, they never can arrive at such a pitch of vivacity, as to render these perceptions altogether undistinguishable. All the colours of poetry, however splendid, can never paint natural objects in such a manner as to make the description be taken for a real landskip. The most lively thought is still inferior to the dullest sensation.

We may observe a like distinction to run through all the other perceptions of the mind. A man in a fit of anger, is actuated in a very different manner from one who only thinks of that emotion. If you tell me, that any person is in love, I easily understand your meaning, and form a just conception of his situation; but never can mistake that conception for the real disorders and agitations of the passion. When we reflect on our past sentiments and affections, our thought is a faithful mirror, and copies its objects truly; but the colours which it employs are faint and dull, in comparison of those in which our original perceptions were clothed. It requires no nice discernment or metaphysical head to mark the distinction between them.

Here therefore we may divide all the perceptions of the mind into two classes or species, which are distinguished by their different degrees of force and vivacity. The less forcible and lively are commonly denominated THOUGHTS or IDEAS. The other species want a name in our language, and in most others; I suppose, because it was not requisite for any, but philosophical purposes, to rank them under a general term or appellation. Let us, therefore, use a little freedom, and call them IMPRESSIONS; employing that word in a sense somewhat different from the usual. By the term *impression*, then, I mean all our more lively perceptions, when we hear, or see, or feel, or love, or hate, or desire, or will. And impressions are distinguished from ideas, which are the less lively perceptions, of which we are conscious, when we reflect on any of those sensations or movements above mentioned.

Nothing, at first view, may seem more unbounded than the thought of man, which not only escapes all human power and authority, but is not even restrained within the limits of nature and reality. To form monsters, and join incongruous shapes and appearances, costs the imagination no more trouble than to conceive the most natural and familiar objects. And while the body is confined to one planet, along which it creeps with pain and difficulty; the thought can in an instant transport us into the most distant regions of the universe; or even beyond the universe, into the unbounded chaos, where nature is supposed to lie in total confusion. What never was seen, or heard of, may yet be conceived; nor is any thing beyond the power of thought, except what implies an absolute contradiction.

But though our thought seems to possess this unbounded liberty, we shall find, upon a nearer examination, that it is really confined within very narrow limits, and that all this creative power of the mind amounts to no more than the faculty of compounding, transposing, augmenting, or diminishing the materials afforded us by the senses and experience. When we think of a golden mountain, we only join two consistent ideas, *gold* and *mountain*, with which we were formerly acquainted. A virtuous horse we can conceive; because, from our own feeling, we can conceive virtue; and this we may unite to the figure and shape of a horse, which is an animal familiar to us. In short, all the materials of thinking are derived either from our outward or inward sentiment: The mixture and composition of these belongs alone to the mind and will. Or, to express myself in philosophical language, all our ideas or more feeble perceptions are copies of our impressions or more lively ones.

To prove this, the two following arguments will, I hope, be sufficient. First, when we analyse our thoughts or ideas, however compounded or sublime, we always find, that they resolve themselves into such simple ideas as were copied from a precedent feeling or sentiment. Even those ideas, which, at first view, seem the most wide of this origin, are found, upon a nearer scrutiny, to be derived from it. The idea of God, as meaning an infinitely intelligent, wise, and good Being, arises from reflecting on the operations of our own mind, and augmenting, without limit, those qualities of goodness and wisdom. We may prosecute this enquiry to what length we please; where we shall always find, that every idea which we examine is copied from a similar impression. Those who would assert, that this position is not universally true nor without exception, have only one, and that an easy method of refuting it; by producing that idea, which, in their opinion, is not derived from this source. It will then be incumbent on us, if we would maintain our doctrine, to produce the impression or lively perception, which corresponds to it.

Secondly. If it happen, from a defect of the organ, that a man is not susceptible of any species of sensation, we always find, that he is as little susceptible of the correspondent ideas. A blind man can form no notion of colours; a deaf man of sounds. Restore either of them that sense, in which he is deficient; by opening this new inlet for his sensations, you also open an inlet for the ideas; and he finds no difficulty in conceiving these objects. The case is the same, if the object, proper for exciting any sensation, has never been applied to the organ. A LAPLANDER or NEGRO has no notion of the relish of wine. And though there are few or no instances of a like deficiency in the mind, where a person has never felt or is wholly incapable of a sentiment or passion, that belongs to his species; yet we find the same observation to take place in a less degree. A man of mild manners can form no idea of inveterate revenge or cruelty; nor can a selfish heart easily conceive the heights of friendship and generosity. It is readily allowed, that other beings may possess many senses of which we can have no conception; because the ideas of them have never been introduced to us, in the only manner, by which an idea can have access to the mind, to wit, by the actual feeling and sensation.

There is, however, one contradictory phenomenon, which may prove, that it is not absolutely impossible for ideas to arise, independent of their correspondent impressions. I believe it will readily be allowed, that the several distinct ideas of colour, which enter by the eye, or those of sound, which are conveyed by the ear, are really different from each other; though, at the same time, resembling. Now if this be true of different colours, it must be no less so of the different shades of the same colour; and each shade produces a distinct idea, independent of the rest. For if this should be denied, it is possible, by the continual gradation of shades, to run a colour insensibly into what is most remote from it; and if you will not allow any of the means to be different, you cannot, without absurdity, deny the extremes to be the same. Suppose, therefore, a person to have enjoyed his sight for thirty years, and to have become perfectly acquainted with colours of all kinds, except one particular shade of blue, for instance, which it never has been his fortune to meet with. Let all the different shades of that colour, except that single one, be placed before him, descending gradually from the deepest to the lightest; it is plain, that he will perceive a blank, where that shade is wanting, and will be sensible, that there is a greater distance in that place between the contiguous colours than in any other. Now I ask, whether it be possible for him, from his own imagination, to supply this deficiency, and raise up to himself the idea of that particular shade, though it had never been conveyed to him by his senses? I believe there are few but will be of opinion that he can: And this may serve as a proof, that the simple ideas are not always, in every instance, derived from the correspondent impressions; though this instance is so singular, that it is scarcely worth our observing, and does not merit, that for it alone we should alter our general maxim.

Here, therefore, is a proposition, which not only seems, in itself, simple and intelligible; but, if a proper use were made of it, might render every dispute equally intelligible, and banish all that jargon, which has so long taken possession of metaphysical reasonings, and drawn disgrace upon them. All ideas, especially abstract ones, are naturally faint and obscure: The mind has but a slender hold of them: They are apt to be confounded with other resembling ideas; and when we have often employed any term, though without a distinct meaning, we are apt to imagine it has a determinate idea, annexed to it. On the contrary, all impressions, that is, all sensations, either outward or inward, are strong and vivid: The limits between them are more exactly determined: Nor is it easy to fall into any error or mistake with regard to them. When we entertain, therefore, any suspicion, that a philosophical term is employed without any meaning or idea (as is but too frequent), we need but enquire, *from what impression is that supposed idea derived?* And if it be impossible to assign any, this will serve to confirm our suspicion. By bringing ideas into so clear a light, we may reasonably hope to remove all dispute, which may arise, concerning their nature and reality.

SECTION III

Of the Association of Ideas

It is evident, that there is a principle of connexion between the different thoughts or ideas of the mind, and that, in their appearance to the memory or imagination, they introduce each other with a certain degree of method and regularity. In our more serious thinking or discourse, this is so observable, that any particular thought, which breaks in upon the regular tract or chain of ideas, is immediately remarked and rejected. And even in our wildest and most wandering reveries, nay in our very dreams, we shall find, if we reflect, that the imagination ran not altogether at adventures, but that there was still a connexion upheld among the different ideas, which succeeded each other. Were the loosest and freest conversation to be transcribed, there would immediately be observed something, which connected it in all its transitions. Or where this is wanting, the person, who broke the thread of discourse, might still inform you, that there had secretly revolved in his mind a succession of thought, which had gradually led him from the subject of conversation. Among different languages, even where we cannot suspect the least connexion or communication, it is found, that the words, expressive of ideas, the most compounded, do yet nearly correspond to each other: A certain proof, that the simple ideas, comprehended in the compound ones, were bound together by some universal principle, which had an equal influence on all mankind.

Though it be too obvious to escape observation, that different ideas are connected together; I do not find, that any philosopher has attempted to enumerate or class all the principles of association; a subject, however, that seems worthy of curiosity. To me, there appear to be only three principles of connexion among ideas, namely, *Resemblance, Contiguity* in time or place, and *Cause* or *Effect.*

That these principles serve to connect ideas will not, I believe, be much doubted. A picture naturally leads our thoughts to the original: The mention of one apartment in a building naturally introduces an enquiry or discourse concerning the others: And if we think of a wound, we can scarcely forbear reflecting on the pain which follows it. But that this enumeration is complete, and that there are no other principles of association, except these, may be difficult to prove to the satisfaction of the reader, or even to a man's own satisfaction. All we can do, in such cases, is to run over several instances, and examine carefully the principle, which binds the different thoughts to each other, never stopping till we render the principle as general as possible. The more instances we examine, and the more care we employ, the more assurance shall we acquire, that the enumeration, which we form from the whole, is complete and entire.

(pp. 20–31)

SECTION IV

Sceptical Doubts

PART II

But we have not, yet, attained any tolerable satisfaction with regard to the question first proposed. Each solution still gives rise to a new question as difficult as the foregoing, and leads us on to farther enquiries. When it is asked, *What is the nature of all our reasonings concerning matter of fact?* the proper answer seems to be, that they are founded on the relation of cause and effect. When again it is asked, *What is the foundation of all our reasonings and conclusions concerning that relation?* it may be replied in one word, EXPERIENCE. But if we still carry on our sifting humour, and ask, *What is the foundation of all conclusions from experience?* this implies a new question, which may be of more difficult solution and explication. Philosophers, that give themselves airs of superior wisdom and sufficiency, have a hard task, when they encounter persons of inquisitive dispositions, who push them from every corner, to which they retreat, and who are sure at last to bring them to some dangerous dilemma. The best expedient to prevent this confusion, is to be modest in our pretensions; and even to discover the difficulty ourselves before it is objected to us. By this means, we may make a kind of merit of our very ignorance.

I shall content myself, in this section, with an easy task, and shall pretend only to give a negative answer to the question here proposed. I say then, that, even after we have experience of the operations of cause and effect, our conclusions from that experience are *not* founded on reasoning, or any process of the understanding. This answer we must endeavour, both to explain and to defend.

It must certainly be allowed, that nature has kept us at a great distance from all her secrets, and has afforded us only the knowledge of a few superficial qualities of objects; while she conceals from us those powers and principles, on which the influence of these objects entirely depends. Our senses inform us of the colour, weight, and consistence of bread; but neither sense nor reason can ever inform us of those qualities, which fit it for the nourishment and support of a human body. Sight or feeling conveys an idea of the actual motion of bodies; but as to that wonderful force or power, which would carry on a moving body for ever in a continued change of place, and which bodies never lose but by communicating it to others; of this we cannot form the most distant conception. But notwithstanding this ignorance of natural powers and principles, we always presume, when we see like sensible qualities, that they have like secret powers, and expect, that effects, similar to those which we have experienced, will follow from them. If a body of like colour and consistence with that bread, which we have formerly eaten, be presented to us, we make no scruple of repeating the experiment, and foresee, with certainty, like nourishment and support. Now this is a process of the mind or thought, of which I would willingly know the foundation. It is allowed on all hands, that there is no known connexion between the sensible qualities and the secret powers; and consequently, that the mind is not led to form such a conclusion concerning their constant and regular conjunction, by any thing which it knows of their nature. As to past *Experience*, it can be allowed to give *direct* and *certain* information of those precise objects only, and that precise period of time, which fell under its cognizance: But why this experience should be extended to future times, and to other objects, which for aught we know, may be only in appearance similar; this is the main question on which I would insist. The bread, which I formerly eat, nourished me; that is, a body of such sensible qualities, was, at that time, endued with such secret powers: But does it follow, that other bread must also nourish me at another time, and that like sensible qualities must always be attended with like secret powers? The consequence seems nowise necessary. At least, it must be acknowledged, that there is here a consequence drawn by the mind; that there is a certain step taken; a process of thought, and an inference, which wants to be explained. These two propositions are far from being the same. *I have found that such an object has always been attended with such an effect*, and *I foresee, that other objects, which are, in appearance, similar, will be attended with similar effects*. I shall allow, if you please, that the one proposition may justly be inferred from the other: I know in fact, that it always is inferred. But if you insist, that the inference is made by a chain of reasoning, I desire you to produce that reasoning. The connexion between these propositions is not intuitive. There is required a medium, which may enable the mind to draw such an inference, if indeed it be drawn by reasoning and argument. What that medium is, I must confess, passes my comprehension; and it is incumbent on those to produce it, who assert, that it really exists, and is the origin of all our conclusions concerning matter of fact.

This negative argument must certainly, in process of time, become altogether convincing, if many penetrating and able philosophers shall turn their enquiries this way; and no one be ever able to discover any connecting proposition or intermediate step, which supports the understanding in this conclusion. But as the question is yet new, every reader may not trust so far to his own penetration, as to conclude, because an argument escapes his enquiry, that therefore it does not really exist. For this reason it may be requisite to venture upon a more difficult task; and enumerating all the branches of human knowledge, endeavour to show, that none of them can afford such an argument.

All reasonings may be divided into two kinds, namely demonstrative reasoning, or that concerning relations of ideas, and moral reasoning, or that concerning matter of fact and existence. That there are no demonstrative arguments in the case, seems evident; since it implies no contradiction, that the course of nature may change, and that an object, seemingly like those which we have experienced, may be attended with different or contrary effects. May I not clearly and distinctly conceive, that a body, falling from the clouds, and which, in all other respects, resembles snow, has yet the taste of salt or feeling of fire? Is there any more intelligible proposition than to affirm, that all the trees will flourish in DECEMBER and JANUARY, and decay in MAY and JUNE? Now whatever is intelligible, and can be distinctly conceived, implies no contradiction, and can never be proved false by any demonstrative argument or abstract reasoning *a priori*.

If we be, therefore, engaged by arguments to put trust in past experience, and make it the standard of our future judgment, these arguments must be probable only, or such as regard matter of fact and real existence, according to the division above mentioned. But that there is no argument of this kind, must appear, if our explication of that species of reasoning be admitted as solid and satisfactory. We have said, that all arguments concerning existence are founded on the relation of cause and effect; that our knowledge of that relation is derived entirely from experience; and that all our experimental conclusions proceed upon the supposition, that the future will be conformable to the past. To endeavour, therefore, the proof of this last supposition by probable arguments, or arguments regarding existence, must be evidently going in a circle, and taking that for granted, which is the very point in question.

In reality, all arguments from experience are founded on the similarity, which we discover among natural objects, and by which we are induced to expect effects similar to those, which we have found to follow from such objects. And though none but a fool or madman will ever pretend to dispute the authority of experience, or to reject that great guide of human life; it may surely be allowed a philosopher to have so much curiosity at least, as to examine the principle of human nature, which gives this mighty authority to experience, and makes us draw advantage from that similarity, which nature has placed among different objects. From causes, which appear *similar*, we expect similar effects. This is the sum of all our experimental conclusions. Now it seems evident, that, if this conclusion were formed by reason, it would be as perfect at first, and upon one instance, as after ever so long a course of experience. But the case is far otherwise. Nothing so like as eggs; yet no one, on account of this appearing similarity, expects the same taste and relish in all of them. It is only after a long course of uniform experiments in any kind, that we attain a firm reliance and security with regard to a particular event. Now where is that process of reasoning, which, from one instance, draws a conclusion, so different from that which it infers from a hundred instances, that are nowise different from that single one? This question I propose as much for the sake of information, as with an intention of raising difficulties. I cannot find, I cannot imagine any such reasoning. But I keep my mind still open to instruction; if any one will vouchsafe to bestow it on me.

Should it be said, that, from a number of uniform experiments, we *infer* a connexion between the sensible qualities and the secret powers; this, I must confess, seems the same difficulty, couched in different terms. The question still recurs, on what process of argument this *inference* is founded? Where is the medium, the interposing ideas, which join propositions so very wide of each other? It is confessed, that the colour, consistence, and other sensible qualities of bread appear not, of themselves, to have any connexion with the secret powers of nourishment and support. For otherwise we could infer these secret powers from the first appearance of these sensible qualities, without the aid of experience; contrary to the sentiment of all philosophers, and contrary to plain matter of fact. Here then is our natural state of ignorance with regard to the powers and influence of all objects. How is this remedied by experience? It only shows us a number of uniform effects, resulting from certain objects, and teaches us, that those particular objects, at that particular time, were endowed with such powers and forces. When a new object, endowed with similar sensible qualities, is produced, we expect similar powers and forces, and look for a like effect. From a body of like colour and consistence with bread, we expect like nourishment and support. But this surely is a step or progress of the mind, which wants to be explained. When a man says, *I have found, in all past instances, such sensible qualities conjoined with such secret powers:* And when he says, *similar sensible qualities will always be conjoined with similar secret powers;* he is not guilty of a tautology, nor are these propositions in any respect the same. You say that the one proposition is an inference from the other. But you must confess that the inference is not intuitive; neither is it demonstrative: Of what nature is it then? To say it is experimental, is begging the question. For all inferences from experience suppose, as their foundation, that the future will resemble the past, and that similar powers will be conjoined with similar sensible qualities. If there be any suspicion, that the course of nature may change, and that the past may be no rule for the future, all experience becomes useless, and can give rise to no inference or conclusion. It is impossible, therefore, that any arguments from experience can prove this resemblance of the past to the future; since all these arguments are founded on the supposition of that resemblance. Let the course of things be allowed hitherto ever so regular; that alone, without some new argument or inference, proves not, that, for the future, it will continue so. In vain do you pretend to have learned the nature of bodies from your past experience. Their secret nature, and consequently, all their effects and influence, may change, without any change in their sensible qualities. This happens sometimes, and with regard to some objects: Why may it not happen always, and with regard to all objects? What logic, what process of argument secures you against this supposition? My practice, you say, refutes my doubts. But you mistake the purport of my question. As an agent, I am quite satisfied in the point; but as a philosopher, who has some share of curiosity, I will not say scepticism, I want to learn the foundation of this inference. No reading, no enquiry has yet been able to remove my difficulty, or give me satisfaction in a matter of such importance. Can I do better than propose the difficulty to the public, even though, perhaps, I have small hopes of obtaining a solution? We shall at least, by this means, be sensible of our ignorance, if we do not augment our knowledge.

I must confess, that a man is guilty of unpardonable arrogance, who concludes, because an argument has escaped his own investigation, that therefore it does not really exist. I must also confess, that, though all the

learned, for several ages, should have employed themselves in fruitless search upon any subject, it may still,
perhaps, be rash to conclude positively, that the subject
must, therefore, pass all human comprehension. Even
though we examine all the sources of our knowledge,
and conclude them unfit for such a subject, there may
still remain a suspicion, that the enumeration is not complete, or the examination not accurate. But with regard to
the present subject, there are some considerations, which
seem to remove all this accusation of arrogance or suspicion of mistake.

It is certain, that the most ignorant and stupid peas-
ants, nay infants, nay even brute beasts, improve by
experience, and learn the qualities of natural objects, by
observing the effects, which result from them. When a
child has felt the sensation of pain from touching the
flame of a candle, he will be careful not to put his hand
near any candle; but will expect a similar effect from a
cause, which is similar in its sensible qualities and
appearance. If you assert, therefore, that the understanding of the child is led into this conclusion by any process
of argument or ratiocination, I may justly require you to
produce that argument; nor have you any pretence to
refuse so equitable a demand. You cannot say, that the
argument is abstruse, and may possibly escape your
enquiry; since you confess, that it is obvious to the
capacity of a mere infant. If you hesitate, therefore, a
moment, or if, after reflection, you produce any intricate
or profound argument, you, in a manner, give up the
question, and confess, that it is not reasoning which
engages us to suppose the past resembling the future,
and to expect similar effects from causes, which are, to
appearance, similar. This is the proposition which I
intended to enforce in the present section. If I be right, I

pretend not to have made any mighty discovery. And if I be wrong, I must acknowledge myself to be indeed a very backward scholar; since I cannot now discover an argument, which, it seems, was perfectly familiar to me, long before I was out of my cradle.

(pp. 25–31)

SECTION V

Sceptical Solution of these Doubts

PART I

THE passion for philosophy, like that for religion, seems liable to this inconvenience, that, though it aims at the correction of our manners, and extirpation of our vices, it may only serve, by imprudent management, to foster a predominant inclination, and push the mind, with more determined resolution, towards that side, which already *draws* too much, by the biass and propensity of the natural temper. It is certain, that, while we aspire to the magnanimous firmness of the philosophic sage, and endeavour to confine our pleasures altogether within our own minds, we may, at last, render our philosophy like that of EPICTETUS, and other *Stoics*, only a more refined system of selfishness, and reason ourselves out of all virtue, as well as social enjoyment. While we study with attention the vanity of human life, and turn all our thoughts towards the empty and transitory nature of riches and honours, we are, perhaps, all the while, flattering our natural indolence, which, hating the bustle of the world, and drudgery of business, seeks a pretence of reason, to give itself a full and uncontrolled indulgence. There is, however, one species of philosophy, which seems little liable to this inconvenience, and that because it strikes in with no disorderly passion of the human mind, nor can mingle itself with any natural affection or propensity; and that is the ACADEMIC or SCEPTICAL philosophy. The academics always talk of doubt and suspense of judgment, of danger in hasty determinations, of confining to very narrow bounds the enquiries of the understanding, and of renouncing all speculations which lie not within the limits of common life and practice. Nothing, therefore, can be more contrary than such a philosophy to the supine indolence of the mind, its rash arrogance, its lofty pretensions, and its superstitious credulity. Every passion is mortified by it, except the love of truth; and that passion never is, nor can be carried to too high a degree. It is surprising, therefore, that this philosophy, which, in almost every instance, must be harmless and innocent, should be the subject of so much groundless reproach and obloquy. But, perhaps, the very circumstance, which renders it so innocent, is what chiefly exposes it to the public hatred and resentment. By flattering no irregular passion, it gains few partizans: By opposing so many vices and follies, it raises to itself abundance of enemies, who stigmatize it as libertine, profane, and irreligious.

Nor need we fear, that this philosophy, while it endeavours to limit our enquiries to common life, should ever undermine the reasonings of common life, and carry its doubts so far as to destroy all action, as well as speculation. Nature will always maintain her rights, and prevail in the end over any abstract reasoning whatsoever. Though we should conclude, for instance, as in the foregoing section, that, in all reasonings from experience, there is a step taken by the mind, which is not supported by any argument or process of the understanding; there is no danger, that these reasonings, on which almost all knowledge depends, will ever be affected by such a discovery. If the mind be not engaged by argument to make this step, it must be induced by some other principle of equal weight and authority; and that principle will preserve its influence as long as human nature remains the same. What that principle is, may well be worth the pains of enquiry.

Suppose a person, though endowed with the strongest faculties of reason and reflection, to be brought on a sudden into this world; he would, indeed, immediately observe a continual succession of objects, and one event following another; but he would not be able to discover any thing farther. He would not, at first, by any reasoning, be able to reach the idea of cause and effect; since the particular powers, by which all natural operations are performed, never appear to the senses; nor is it reasonable to conclude, merely because one event, in one instance, precedes another, that therefore the one is the cause, the other the effect. Their conjunction may be arbitrary and casual. There may be no reason to infer the existence of one from the appearance of the other. And in a word, such a person, without more experience, could never employ his conjecture or reasoning concerning any matter of fact, or be assured of any thing beyond what was immediately present to his memory and senses.

Suppose again, that he has acquired more experience, and has lived so long in the world as to have observed similar objects or events to be constantly conjoined together; what is the consequence of this experience? He immediately infers the existence of one object from the appearance of the other. Yet he has not, by all his experience, acquired any idea or knowledge of the secret power, by which the one object produces the other; nor is it, by any process of reasoning, he is engaged to draw this inference. But still he finds himself determined to draw it: And though he should be convinced, that his understanding has no part in the operation, he would nevertheless continue in the same course of thinking. There is some other principle, which determines him to form such a conclusion.

This principle is CUSTOM or HABIT. For wherever the repetition of any particular act or operation produces a propensity to renew the same act or operation, without being impelled by any reasoning or process of the understanding; we always say, that this propensity is the effect of *Custom*. By employing that word, we pretend not to have given the ultimate reason of such a propensity. We only point out a principle of human nature, which is universally acknowledged, and which is well known by its effects. Perhaps, we can push our enquiries no farther, or pretend to give the cause of this cause; but must rest contented with it as the ultimate principle, which we can assign, of all our conclusions from experience. It is sufficient satisfaction, that we can go so far; without repining at the narrowness of our faculties, because they will carry us no farther. And it is certain we here advance a very intelligible proposition at least, if not a true one, when we assert, that, after the constant conjunction of two objects, heat and flame, for instance, weight and solidity, we are determined by custom alone to expect the one from the appearance of the other. This hypothesis seems even the only one, which explains the difficulty, why we draw, from a thousand instances, an inference, which we are not able to draw from one instance, that is, in no respect, different from them. Reason is incapable of any such variation. The conclusions, which it draws from considering one circle, are the same which it would form upon surveying all the circles in the universe. But no man, having seen only one body move after being impelled by another, could infer, that every other body will move after a like impulse. All inferences from experience, therefore, are effects of custom, not of reasoning.

Custom, then, is the great guide of human life. It is that principle alone, which renders our experience useful to us, and makes us expect, for the future, a similar train of events with those which have appeared in the past. Without the influence of custom, we should be entirely ignorant of every matter of fact, beyond what is immediately present to the memory and senses. We should never know how to adjust means to ends, or to employ our natural powers in the production of any effect. There would be an end at once of all action, as well as of the chief part of speculation.

But here it may be proper to remark, that though our conclusions from experience carry us beyond our memory and senses, and assure us of matters of fact, which happened in the most distant places and most remote ages; yet some fact must always be present to the senses or memory, from which we may first proceed in drawing these conclusions. A man, who should find in a desert country the remains of pompous buildings, would conclude, that the country had, in ancient times, been cultivated by civilized inhabitants; but did nothing of this nature occur to him, he could never form such an inference. We learn the events of former ages from history; but then we must peruse the volumes, in which this instruction is contained, and thence carry up our inferences from one testimony to another, till we arrive at the eye-witnesses and spectators of these distant events. In a word, if we proceed not upon some fact, present to the memory or senses, our reasonings would be merely hypothetical; and however the particular links might be connected with each other, the whole chain of inferences would have nothing to support it, nor could we ever, by its means, arrive at the knowledge of any real existence. If I ask, why you believe any particular matter of fact, which you relate, you must tell me some reason; and this reason will be some other fact, connected with it. But as you cannot proceed after this manner, *in infinitum*, you must at last terminate in some fact, which is present to your memory or senses; or must allow that your belief is entirely without foundation.

What then is the conclusion of the whole matter? A simple one; though, it must be confessed, pretty remote from the common theories of philosophy. All belief of matter of fact or real existence is derived merely from some object, present to the memory or senses, and a customary conjunction between that and some other object. Or in other words; having found, in many instances, that any two kinds of objects, flame and heat, snow and cold, have always been conjoined together; if flame or snow be presented anew to the senses, the mind is carried by custom to expect heat or cold, and to *believe*, that such a quality does exist, and will discover itself upon a nearer approach. This belief is the necessary result of placing the mind in such circumstances. It is an operation of the soul, when we are so situated, as unavoidable as to feel the passion of love, when we receive benefits; or hatred, when we meet with injuries. All these operations are a species of natural instincts, which no reasoning or process of the thought and understanding is able, either to produce, or to prevent.

At this point, it would be very allowable for us to stop our philosophical researches. In most questions, we can never make a single step farther; and in all questions,

we must terminate here at last, after our most restless
and curious enquiries. But still our curiosity will be
pardonable, perhaps commendable, if it carry us on to
still farther researches, and make us examine more accurately the nature of this *belief*, and of the *customary conjunction*, whence it is derived. By this means we may
meet with some explications and analogies, that will give
satisfaction; at least to such as love the abstract sciences,
and can be entertained with speculations, which, however accurate, may still retain a degree of doubt and uncertainty. As to readers of a different taste; the remaining
part of this section is not calculated for them, and the following enquiries may well be understood, though it be
neglected.

(pp. 53–55)

SECTION VIII

Of Liberty and Necessity

PART I

IT might reasonably be expected, in questions, which
have been canvassed and disputed with great eagerness,
since the first origin of science and philosophy, that the
meaning of all the terms, at least, should have been
agreed upon among the disputants; and our enquiries, in
the course of two thousand years, been able to pass from
words to the true and real subject of the controversy. For
how easy may it seem to give exact definitions of the
terms employed in reasoning, and make these definitions,
not the mere sound of words, the object of future scrutiny and examination? But if we consider the matter
more narrowly, we shall be apt to draw a quite opposite

conclusion. From this circumstance alone, that a controversy has been long kept on foot, and remains still undecided, we may presume, that there is some ambiguity in the expression, and that the disputants affix different ideas to the terms employed in the controversy. For as the faculties of the mind are supposed to be naturally alike in every individual; otherwise nothing could be more fruitless than to reason or dispute together; it were impossible, if men affix the same ideas to their terms, that they could so long form different opinions of the same subject; especially when they communicate their views, and each party turn themselves on all sides, in search of arguments, which may give them the victory over their antagonists. It is true; if men attempt the discussion of questions, which lie entirely beyond the reach of human capacity, such as those concerning the origin of worlds, or the economy of the intellectual system or region of spirits, they may long beat the air in their fruitless contests, and never arrive at any determinate conclusion. But if the question regard any subject of common life and experience; nothing, one would think, could preserve the dispute so long undecided, but some ambiguous expressions, which keep the antagonists still at a distance, and hinder them from grappling with each other.

This has been the case in the long disputed question concerning liberty and necessity; and to so remarkable a degree, that, if I be not much mistaken, we shall find, that all mankind, both learned and ignorant, have always been of the same opinion with regard to this subject, and that a few intelligible definitions would immediately have put an end to the whole controversy. I own, that this dispute has been so much canvassed on all hands, and has led philosophers into such a labyrinth of obscure sophistry, that it is no wonder, if a sensible reader

indulge his ease so far as to turn a deaf ear to the proposal of such a question, from which he can expect
neither instruction nor entertainment. But the state of the
argument here proposed may, perhaps, serve to renew
his attention; as it has more novelty, promises at least
some decision of the controversy, and will not much disturb his ease by any intricate or obscure reasoning.

I hope, therefore, to make it appear, that all men
have ever agreed in the doctrine both of necessity and of
liberty, according to any reasonable sense, which can be
put on these terms; and that the whole controversy has
hitherto turned merely upon words. We shall begin with
examining the doctrine of necessity.

It is universally allowed, that matter, in all its operations, is actuated by a necessary force, and that every
natural effect is so precisely determined by the energy of
its cause, that no other effect, in such particular circumstances, could possibly have resulted from it. The degree
and direction of every motion is, by the laws of nature,
prescribed with such exactness, that a living creature may
as soon arise from the shock of two bodies, as motion, in
any other degree or direction than what is actually produced by it. Would we, therefore, form a just and precise
idea of *necessity*, we must consider whence that idea
arises, when we apply it to the operation of bodies.

It seems evident, that, if all the scenes of nature
were continually shifted in such a manner, that no two
events bore any resemblance to each other, but every
object was entirely new, without any similitude to whatever had been seen before, we should never, in that
case, have attained the least idea of necessity, or of a
connexion among these objects. We might say, upon
such a supposition, that one object or event has followed
another; not that one was produced by the other. The

relation of cause and effect must be utterly unknown to mankind. Inference and reasoning concerning the operations of nature would, from that moment, be at an end; and the memory and senses remain the only canals, by which the knowledge of any real existence could possibly have access to the mind. Our idea, therefore, of necessity and causation arises entirely from the uniformity, observable in the operations of nature; where similar objects are constantly conjoined together, and the mind is determined by custom to infer the one from the appearance of the other. These two circumstances form the whole of that necessity, which we ascribe to matter. Beyond the constant *conjunction* of similar objects, and the consequent *inference* from one to the other, we have no notion of any necessity, or connexion.

If it appear, therefore, that all mankind have ever allowed, without any doubt or hesitation, that these two circumstances take place in the voluntary actions of men, and in the operations of mind; it must follow, that all mankind have ever agreed in the doctrine of necessity, and that they have hitherto disputed, merely for not understanding each other.

As to the first circumstance, the constant and regular conjunction of similar events; we may possibly satisfy ourselves by the following considerations. It is universally acknowledged, that there is a great uniformity among the actions of men, in all nations and ages, and that human nature remains still the same, in its principles and operations. The same motives always produce the same actions: The same events follow from the same causes. Ambition, avarice, self-love, vanity, friendship, generosity, public spirit; these passions, mixed in various degrees, and distributed through society, have been, from the beginning of the world, and still are, the source of all the actions and enterprises which have ever been observed among mankind.

▬▬▬▬▬▬▬▬

(pp.61–64)

I have frequently considered, what could possibly be the reason, why all mankind, though they have ever, without hesitation, acknowledged the doctrine of necessity, in their whole practice and reasoning, have yet discovered such a reluctance to acknowledge it in words and have rather shown a propensity, in all ages, to profess the contrary opinion. The matter, I think, may be accounted for, after the following manner. If we examine the operations of body, and the production of effects from their causes, we shall find, that all our faculties can never carry us farther in our knowledge of this relation, than barely to observe, that particular objects are *constantly conjoined* together, and that the mind is carried, by a *customary transition*, from the appearance of one to the belief of the other. But though this conclusion concerning human ignorance be the result of the strictest scrutiny of this subject, men still entertain a strong propensity to believe, that they penetrate farther into the powers of nature, and perceive something like a necessary connexion between the cause and the effect. When again they turn their reflections towards the operations of their own minds, and *feel* no such connexion of the motive and the action; they are thence apt to suppose, that there is a difference between the effects, which result from material force, and those which arise from thought and intelligence. But being once convinced, that we know nothing farther of causation of any kind, than merely the *constant conjunction* of objects, and the consequent *inference* of the mind from one to another, and finding, that these two circumstances are universally allowed to have place in voluntary actions; we may be more easily led to own the same necessity common to all causes. And though this reasoning may contradict the systems of many philosophers, in ascribing necessity to the determinations of the will, we shall find, upon reflection, that they dissent from it in words only, not in their real sentiment. Necessity, according to the sense, in which it is here taken, has never yet been rejected, nor can ever, I think, be rejected by any philosopher. It may only, perhaps, be pretended, that the mind can perceive, in the operations of matter, some farther connexion between the cause and effect; and a connexion that has not place in the voluntary actions of intelligent beings. Now whether it be so or not, can only appear upon examination; and it is incumbent on these philosophers to make good their assertion, by defining or describing that necessity, and pointing it out to us in the operations of material causes.

It would seem, indeed, that men begin at the wrong end of this question concerning liberty and necessity, when they enter upon it by examining the faculties of the soul, the influence of the understanding, and the operations of the will. Let them first discuss a more simple question, namely, the operations of body and of brute unintelligent matter; and try whether they can there form any idea of causation and necessity, except that of a constant conjunction of objects, and subsequent inference of the mind from one to another. If these circumstances form, in reality, the whole of that necessity, which we conceive in matter, and if these circumstances be also universally acknowledged to take place in the operations of the mind, the dispute is at an end; at least, must be owned to be thenceforth merely verbal. But as long as we will rashly suppose, that we have some farther idea

of necessity and causation in the operations of external
objects; at the same time, that we can find nothing
farther, in the voluntary actions of the mind; there is no
possibility of bringing the question to any determinate
issue, while we proceed upon so erroneous a supposition. The only method of undeceiving us, is, to mount up
higher; to examine the narrow extent of science when
applied to material causes; and to convince ourselves,
that all we know of them, is, the constant conjunction
and inference above mentioned. We may, perhaps, find,
that it is with difficulty we are induced to fix such narrow
limits to human understanding: But we can afterwards
find no difficulty when we come to apply this doctrine to
the actions of the will. For as it is evident, that these have
a regular conjunction with motives and circumstances
and characters, and as we always draw inferences from
one to the other, we must be obliged to acknowledge in
words, that necessity, which we have already avowed, in
every deliberation of our lives, and in every step of our
conduct and behaviour.

But to proceed in this reconciling project with
regard to the question of liberty and necessity; the most
contentious question, of metaphysics, the most contentious science; it will not require many words to prove,
that all mankind have ever agreed in the doctrine of liberty as well as in that of necessity, and that the whole
dispute, in this respect also, has been hitherto merely
verbal. For what is meant by liberty, when applied to
voluntary actions? We cannot surely mean, that actions
have so little connexion with motives, inclinations, and
circumstances, that one does not follow with a certain
degree of uniformity from the other, and that one affords
no inference by which we can conclude the existence of
the other. For these are plain and acknowledged matters

of fact. By liberty, then, we can only mean *a power of acting or not acting, according to the determinations of the will;* that is, if we choose to remain at rest, we may; if we choose to move, we also may. Now this hypothetical liberty is universally allowed to belong to every one, who is not a prisoner and in chains. Here then is no subject of dispute.

Whatever definition we may give of liberty, we should be careful to observe two requisite circumstances; *first*, that it be consistent with plain matter of fact; *secondly*, that it be consistent with itself. If we observe these circumstances, and render our definition intelligible, I am persuaded that all mankind will be found of one opinion with regard to it.

It is universally allowed, that nothing exists without a cause of its existence, and that chance, when strictly examined, is a mere negative word, and means not any real power, which has any where, a being in nature. But it is pretended, that some causes are necessary, some not necessary. Here then is the advantage of definitions. Let any one *define* a cause, without comprehending, as a part of the definition, a *necessary connexion* with its effect; and let him show distinctly the origin of the idea, expressed by the definition; and I shall readily give up the whole controversy. But if the foregoing explication of the matter be received, this must be absolutely impracticable. Had not objects a regular conjunction with each other, we should never have entertained any notion of cause and effect; and this regular conjunction produces that inference of the understanding, which is the only connexion, that we can have any comprehension of. Whoever attempts a definition of cause, exclusive of these circumstances, will be obliged, either to employ unintelligible terms, or such as are synonymous to the

term, which he endeavours to define. And if the definition above mentioned be admitted; liberty, when
opposed to necessity, not to constraint, is the same thing
with chance; which is universally allowed to have no
existence.

▬▬▬▬▬▬▬▬▬▬▬▬

(pp. 72–77)

SECTION X
Of Miracles
PART I

THERE is, in DR. TILLOTSON'S writings, an argument against
the *real presence*, which is as concise, and elegant, and
strong as any argument can possibly be supposed against
a doctrine, so little worthy of a serious refutation. It is
acknowledged on all hands, says that learned prelate,
that the authority, either of the scripture or of tradition, is
founded merely in the testimony of the apostles, who
were eye-witnesses to those miracles of our Saviour, by
which he proved his divine mission. Our evidence, then,
for the truth of the *Christian* religion is less than the evidence for the truth of our senses; because, even in the
first authors of our religion, it was no greater; and it is
evident it must diminish in passing from them to their
disciples; nor can any one rest such confidence in their
testimony, as in the immediate object of his senses. But
a weaker evidence can never destroy a stronger; and
therefore, were the doctrine of the real presence ever so
clearly revealed in scripture, it were directly contrary to
the rules of just reasoning to give our assent to it. It
contradicts sense, though both the scripture and tradition, on which it is supposed to be built, carry not such

evidence with them as sense; when they are considered merely as external evidences, and are not brought home to every one's breast, by the immediate operation of the Holy Spirit.

Nothing is so convenient as a decisive argument of this kind, which must at least *silence* the most arrogant bigotry and superstition, and free us from their impertinent solicitations. I flatter myself, that I have discovered an argument of a like nature, which, if just, will, with the wise and learned, be an everlasting check to all kinds of superstitious delusion, and consequently, will be useful as long as the world endures. For so long, I presume, will the accounts of miracles and prodigies be found in all history, sacred and profane.

Though experience be our only guide in reasoning concerning matters of fact; it must be acknowledged, that this guide is not altogether infallible, but in some cases is apt to lead us into errors. One, who in our climate, should expect better weather in any week of JUNE than in one of DECEMBER, would reason justly, and conformably to experience; but it is certain, that he may happen, in the event, to find himself mistaken. However, we may observe, that, in such a case, he would have no cause to complain of experience; because it commonly informs us beforehand of the uncertainty, by that contrariety of events, which we may learn from a diligent observation. All effects follow not with like certainty from their supposed causes. Some events are found, in all countries and all ages, to have been constantly conjoined together. Others are found to have been more variable, and sometimes to disappoint our expectations; so that, in our reasonings concerning matter of fact, there are all imaginable degrees of assurance, from the highest certainty to the lowest species of moral evidence.

A wise man, therefore, proportions his belief to the evidence. In such conclusions as are founded on an infallible experience, he expects the event with the last degree of assurance, and regards his past experience as a full *proof* of the future existence of that event. In other cases, he proceeds with more caution: He weighs the opposite experiments: He considers which side is supported by the greater number of experiments: To that side he inclines, with doubt and hesitation; and when at last he fixes his judgment, the evidence exceeds not what we properly call *probability*. A probability, then, supposes an opposition of experiments and observations, where the one side is found to overbalance the other, and to produce a degree of evidence, proportioned to the superiority. A hundred instances or experiments on one side, and fifty on another, afford a doubtful expectation of any event; though a hundred uniform experiments, with only one that is contradictory, reasonably beget a pretty strong degree of assurance. In all cases, we must balance the opposite experiments, where they are opposite, and deduct the smaller number from the greater, in order to know the exact force of the superior evidence.

To apply these principles to a particular instance; we may observe, that there is no species of reasoning more common, more useful, and even necessary to human life, than that which is derived from the testimony of men, and the reports of eye-witnesses and spectators. This species of reasoning, perhaps, one may deny to be founded on the relation of cause and effect. I shall not dispute about a word. It will be sufficient to observe, that our assurance in any argument of this kind is derived from no other principle than our observation of the veracity of human testimony, and of the usual conformity of facts to the reports of witnesses. It being a general maxim, that no objects have any discoverable connexion together, and that all the inferences, which we can draw from one to another, are founded merely on our experience of their constant and regular conjunction; it is evident, that we ought not to make an exception to this maxim in favour of human testimony, whose connexion with any event seems, in itself, as little necessary as any other. Were not the memory tenacious to a certain degree; had not men commonly an inclination to truth and a principle of probity; were they not sensible to shame, when detected in a falsehood: Were not these, I say, discovered by *experience* to be qualities, inherent in human nature, we should never repose the least confidence in human testimony. A man delirious, or noted for falsehood and villainy, has no manner of authority with us.

And as the evidence, derived from witnesses and human testimony, is founded on past experience, so it varies with the experience, and is regarded either as a *proof* or a *probability*, according as the conjunction between any particular kind of report and any kind of object has been found to be constant or variable. There are a number of circumstances to be taken into consideration in all judgments of this kind; and the ultimate standard, by which we determine all disputes, that may arise concerning them, is always derived from experience and observation. Where this experience is not entirely uniform on any side, it is attended with an unavoidable contrariety in our judgments, and with the same opposition and mutual destruction of argument as in every other kind of evidence. We frequently hesitate concerning the reports of others. We balance the opposite circumstances, which cause any doubt or uncertainty; and when we discover a superiority on any side, we incline to it; but still with a diminution of assurance, in proportion to the force of its antagonist.

This contrariety of evidence, in the present case, may be derived from several different causes; from the opposition of contrary testimony; from the character or number of the witnesses; from the manner of their delivering their testimony; or from the union of all these circumstances. We entertain a suspicion concerning any matter of fact, when the witnesses contradict each other; when they are but few, or of a doubtful character; when they have an interest in what they affirm; when they deliver their testimony with hesitation, or on the contrary, with too violent asseverations. There are many other particulars of the same kind, which may diminish or destroy the force of any argument, derived from human testimony.

Suppose, for instance, that the fact, which the testimony endeavours to establish, partakes of the extraordinary and the marvellous; in that case, the evidence, resulting from the testimony, admits of a diminution, greater or less, in proportion as the fact is more or less unusual. The reason, why we place any credit in witnesses and historians, is not derived from any *connexion*, which we perceive *a priori*, between testimony and reality, but because we are accustomed to find a conformity between them. But when the fact attested is such a one as has seldom fallen under our observation, here is a contest of two opposite experiences; of which the one destroys the other, as far as its force goes, and the superior can only operate on the mind by the force, which remains. The very same principle of experience, which gives us a certain degree of assurance in the testimony of witnesses, gives us also, in this case, another degree of assurance against the fact, which they endeavour to establish; from which contradiction there necessarily arises a counterpoise, and mutual destruction of belief and authority.

I should not believe such a story were it told me by CATO; was a proverbial saying in ROME, even during the lifetime of that philosophical patriot. The incredibility of a fact, it was allowed, might invalidate so great an authority.

The INDIAN prince, who refused to believe the first relations concerning the effects of frost, reasoned justly; and it naturally required very strong testimony to engage his assent to facts, that arose from a state of nature, with which he was unacquainted, and which bore so little analogy to those events, of which he had had constant and uniform experience. Though they were not contrary to his experience, they were not conformable to it.

But in order to increase the probability against the testimony of witnesses, let us suppose, that the fact, which they affirm, instead of being only marvellous, is really miraculous; and suppose also, that the testimony, considered apart and in itself, amounts to an entire proof; in that case, there is proof against proof, of which the strongest must prevail, but still with a diminution of its force, in proportion to that of its antagonist.

A miracle is a violation of the laws of nature; and as a firm and unalterable experience has established these laws, the proof against a miracle, from the very nature of the fact, is as entire as any argument from experience can possibly be imagined. Why is it more than probable, that all men must die; that lead cannot, of itself, remain suspended in the air; that fire consumes wood, and is extinguished by water; unless it be, that these events are found agreeable to the laws of nature, and there is required a violation of these laws, or in other words, a miracle to prevent them? Nothing is esteemed a miracle, if it ever happen in the common course of nature. It is no miracle that a man, seemingly in good health, should die on a sudden: because such a kind of death, though more unusual than any other, has yet been frequently observed to happen. But it is a miracle, that a dead man should come to life; because that has never been observed, in any age or country. There must, therefore, be a uniform experience against every miraculous event, otherwise the event would not merit that appellation. And as an uniform experience amounts to a proof, there is here a direct and full *proof*, from the nature of the fact, against the existence of any miracle; nor can such a proof be destroyed, or the miracle rendered credible, but by an opposite proof, which is superior.

The plain consequence is (and it is a general maxim worthy of our attention), 'That no testimony is sufficient to establish a miracle, unless the testimony be of such a kind, that its falsehood would be more miraculous, than the fact, which it endeavours to establish: And even in that case there is a mutual destruction of arguments, and the superior only gives us an assurance suitable to that degree of force, which remains, after deducting the inferior.' When any one tells me, that he saw a dead man restored to life, I immediately consider with myself, whether it be more probable, that this person should either deceive or be deceived, or that the fact, which he relates, should really have happened. I weigh the one miracle against the other; and according to the superiority, which I discover, I pronounce my decision, and always reject the greater miracle. If the falsehood of his testimony would be more miraculous, than the event which he relates; then, and not till then, can he pretend to command my belief or opinion.

Dialogues Concerning Natural Religion

ed. Norman Kemp Smith.
New York: Bobbs-Merill, 1947.

(pp. 214–28)

PART XII

AFTER DEMEA'S departure, CLEANTHES and PHILO continued the conversation in the following manner. Our friend, I am afraid, said CLEANTHES, will have little inclination to revive this topic of discourse, while you are in company; and to tell truth, PHILO, I should rather wish to reason with either of you apart on a subject so sublime and interesting. Your spirit of controversy, joined to your abhorrence of vulgar superstition, carries you strange lengths, when engaged in an argument; and there is nothing so sacred and venerable, even in your own eyes, which you spare on that occasion.

I must confess, replied PHILO, that I am less cautious on the subject of natural religion than on any other; both because I know that I can never, on that head, corrupt the principles of any man of common sense, and because no one, I am confident, in whose eyes I appear a man of common sense, will ever mistake my intentions.

You, in particular, CLEANTHES, with whom I live in unreserved intimacy; you are sensible, that, notwithstanding the freedom of my conversation, and my love of singular arguments, no one has a deeper sense of religion impressed on his mind, or pays more profound adoration to the divine Being, as he discovers himself to reason, in the inexplicable contrivance and artifice of nature. A purpose, an intention, or design strikes everywhere the most careless, the most stupid thinker; and no man can be so hardened in absurd systems, as at all times to reject it. *That nature does nothing in vain*, is a maxim established in all the schools, merely from the contemplation of the works of nature, without any religious purpose; and, from a firm conviction of its truth, an anatomist, who had observed a new organ or canal, would never be satisfied till he had also discovered its use and intention. One great foundation of the COPERNICAN system is the maxim, *that nature acts by the simplest methods, and chooses the most proper means to any end;* and astronomers often, without thinking of it, lay this strong foundation of piety and religion. [The same thing is observable in other parts of philosophy: And] thus all the sciences almost lead us insensibly to acknowledge a first intelligent Author; and their authority is often so much the greater, as they do not directly profess that intention.

It is with pleasure I hear GALEN reason concerning the structure of the human body. The anatomy of a man, says he, discovers above 600 different muscles; and whoever duly considers these, will find, that in each of them nature must have adjusted at least ten different circumstances, in order to attain the end which she proposed; proper figure, just magnitude, right disposition of the several ends, upper and lower position of the whole, the due insertion of the several nerves, veins, and arteries: So that, in the muscles alone, above 6,000 several views and intentions must have been formed and executed. The bones he calculates to be 284: The distinct purposes, aimed at in the structure of each, above forty. What a prodigious display of artifice, even in these simple and homogeneous parts? But if we consider the skin, ligaments, vessels, glandules, humours, the several limbs and members of the body; how must our astonishment rise upon us, in proportion to the number and intricacy of the parts so artificially adjusted? The farther we advance in these researches, we discover new scenes of art and wisdom: But descry still, at a distance, farther scenes beyond our reach; in the fine internal structure of the parts, in the œconomy of the brain, in the fabric of the seminal vessels. All these artifices are repeated in every different species of animal, with wonderful variety, and with exact propriety, suited to the different intentions of nature, in framing each species. And if the infidelity of GALEN, even when these natural sciences were still imperfect, could not withstand such striking appearances; to what pitch of pertinacious obstinacy must a philosopher in this age have attained, who can now doubt of a supreme intelligence?

Could I meet with one of this species (who, I thank God, are very rare) I would ask him: Supposing there were a God, who did not discover himself immediately to our senses; were it possible for him to give stronger proofs of his existence, than what appear on the whole face of nature? What indeed could such a divine Being do, but copy the present œconomy of things; render many of his artifices so plain, that no stupidity could mistake them; afford glimpses of still greater artifices, which demonstrate his prodigious superiority above our narrow apprehensions; and conceal altogether a great many from such imperfect creatures? Now according to all rules of just reasoning, every fact must pass for undisputed, when it is supported by all the arguments which its nature admits of, even though these arguments be not, in themselves, very numerous or forcible: How much more, in the present case, where no human imagination can compute their number, and no understanding estimate their cogency?

I shall farther add, said CLEANTHES, to what you have so well urged, that one great advantage of the principle of theism, is, that it is the only system of cosmogony which can be rendered intelligible and complete, and yet can throughout preserve a strong analogy to what we every day see and experience in the world. The comparison of the universe to a machine of human contrivance is so obvious and natural, and is justified by so many instances of order and design in nature, that it must immediately strike all unprejudiced apprehensions, and procure universal approbation. Whoever attempts to weaken this theory, cannot pretend to succeed by establishing in its place any other that is precise and determinate: It is sufficient for him, if he start doubts and difficulties; and by remote and abstract views of things, reach that suspence of judgment, which is here the utmost boundary of his wishes. But besides that this state of mind is in itself unsatisfactory, it can never be steadily maintained against such striking appearances as continually engage us into the religious hypothesis. A false, absurd system, human nature, from the force of prejudice, is capable of adhering to with obstinacy and perseverance: But no system at all, in opposition to a theory, supported by strong and obvious reason, by natural propensity, and by early education, I think it absolutely impossible to maintain or defend.

So little, replied PHILO, do I esteem this suspense of judgment in the present case to be possible, that I am apt to suspect there enters somewhat of a dispute of words into this controversy, more than is usually imagined. That the works of nature bear a great analogy to the productions of art is evident; and according to all the rules of good reasoning, we ought to infer, if we argue at all concerning them, that their causes have a proportional analogy. But as there are also considerable differences, we have reason to suppose a proportional difference in the causes; and in particular ought to attribute a much higher degree of power and energy to the supreme cause than any we have ever observed in mankind. Here then the existence of a DEITY is plainly ascertained by reason; and if we make it a question, whether, on account of these analogies, we can properly call him a *mind* or *intelligence*, notwithstanding the vast difference, which may reasonably be supposed between him and human minds; what is this but a mere verbal controversy? No man can deny the analogies between the effects: To restrain ourselves from enquiring concerning the causes is scarcely possible: From this enquiry, the legitimate conclusion is, that the causes have also an analogy: And if we are not contented with calling the first and supreme cause a GOD or DEITY, but desire to vary the expression; what can we call him but MIND or THOUGHT, to which he is justly supposed to bear a considerable resemblance?

All men of sound reason are disgusted with verbal disputes, which abound so much in philosophical and theological enquiries; and it is found, that the only remedy for this abuse must arise from clear definitions, from the precision of those ideas which enter into any argument, and from the strict and uniform use of those terms which are employed. But there is a species of

controversy, which, from the very nature of language and
of human ideas, is involved in perpetual ambiguity, and
can never, by any precaution or any definitions, be able
to reach a reasonable certainty or precision. These are
the controversies concerning the degrees of any quality
or circumstance. Men may argue to all eternity, whether
Hannibal be a great, or a very great, or superlatively
great man, what degree of beauty Cleopatra possessed,
what epithet of praise Livy or Thucydides is entitled to,
without bringing the controversy to any determination.
The disputants may here agree in their sense and differ
in the terms, or *vice versa*; yet never be able to define
their terms, so as to enter into each other's meaning:
Because the degrees of these qualities are not, like quan-
tity or number, susceptible of any exact mensuration,
which may be the standard in the controversy. That the
dispute concerning theism is of this nature, and consequently is merely verbal, or perhaps, if possible, still
more incurably ambiguous, will appear upon the slight-
est enquiry. I ask the theist, if he does not allow, that
there is a great and immeasurable, because incomprehensible, difference between the *human* and the *divine*
mind: The more pious he is, the more readily will he
assent to the affirmative, and the more will he be disposed to magnify the difference: He will even assert, that
the difference is of a nature which cannot be too much
magnified. I next turn to the atheist, who, I assert, is only
nominally so, and can never possibly be in earnest; and I
ask him, whether, from the coherence and apparent sympathy in all the parts of this world, there be not a certain
degree of analogy among all the operations of nature, in
every situation and in every age; whether the rotting of a
turnip, the generation of an animal, and the structure of
human thought be not energies that probably bear some

remote analogy to each other: It is impossible he can deny it: He will readily acknowledge it. Having obtained this concession, I push him still farther in his retreat; and I ask him, if it be not probable, that the principle which first arranged, and still maintains, order in this universe, bears not also some remote inconceivable analogy to the other operations of nature, and among the rest to the œconomy of human mind and thought. However reluctant, he must give his assent. Where then, cry I to both these antagonists, is the subject of your dispute? The theist allows, that the original intelligence is very different from human reason: The atheist allows, that the original principle of order bears some remote analogy to it. Will you quarrel, Gentlemen, about the degrees, and enter into a controversy, which admits not of any precise meaning, nor consequently of any determination? If you should be so obstinate, I should not be surprised to find you insensibly change sides; while the theist on the one hand exaggerates the dissimilarity between the supreme Being, and frail, imperfect, variable, fleeting, and mortal creatures; and the atheist on the other magnifies the analogy among all the operations of nature, in every period, every situation, and every position. Consider then, where the real point of controversy lies, and if you cannot lay aside your disputes, endeavour, at least, to cure yourselves of your animosity.

And here I must also acknowledge, CLEANTHES, that, as the works of nature have a much greater analogy to the effects of *our* art and contrivance, than to those of *our* benevolence and justice; we have reason to infer that the natural attributes of the Deity have a greater resemblance to those of man, than his moral have to human virtues. But what is the consequence? Nothing but this, that the moral qualities of man are more defective in their kind than his natural abilities. For, as the supreme Being is allowed to be absolutely and entirely perfect, whatever differs most from him departs the farthest from the supreme standard of rectitude and perfection.

These, CLEANTHES, are my unfeigned sentiments on this subject; and these sentiments, you know, I have ever cherished and maintained. But in proportion to my veneration for true religion, is my abhorrence of vulgar superstitions; and I indulge a peculiar pleasure, I confess, in pushing such principles, sometimes into absurdity, sometimes into impiety. And you are sensible, that all bigots, notwithstanding their great aversion to the latter above the former, are commonly equally guilty of both.

My inclination, replied CLEANTHES, lies, I own, a contrary way. Religion, however corrupted, is still better than no religion at all. The doctrine of a future state is so strong and necessary a security to morals, that we never ought to abandon or neglect it. For if finite and temporary rewards and punishments have so great an effect, as we daily find: How much greater must be expected from such as are infinite and eternal?

How happens it then, said PHILO, if vulgar superstition be so salutary to society, that all history abounds so much with accounts of its pernicious consequences on public affairs? Factions, civil wars, persecutions, subversions of government, oppression, slavery; these are the dismal consequences which always attend its prevalency over the minds of men. If the religious spirit be ever mentioned in any historical narration, we are sure to meet afterwards with a detail of the miseries which attend it. And no period of time can be happier or more prosperous, than those in which it is never regarded, or heard of.

The reason of this observation, replied CLEANTHES, is obvious. The proper office of religion is to regulate the heart of men, humanize their conduct, infuse the spirit of temperance, order, and obedience; and as its operation is silent, and only enforces the motives of mortality and justice, it is in danger of being overlooked, and confounded with these other motives. When it distinguishes itself, and acts as a separate principle over men, it has departed from its proper sphere, and has become only a cover to faction and ambition.

And so will all religion, said PHILO, except the philosophical and rational kind. Your reasonings are more easily eluded than my facts. The inference is not just, because finite and temporary rewards and punishments have so great influence, that therefore such as are infinite and eternal must have so much greater. Consider, I beseech you, the attachment, which we have to present things, and the little concern which we discover for objects so remote and uncertain. When divines are declaiming against the common behaviour and conduct of the world, they always represent this principle as the strongest imaginable (which indeed it is) and describe almost all human kind as lying under the influence of it, and sunk into the deepest lethargy and unconcern about their religious interests. Yet these same divines, when they refute their speculative antagonists, suppose the motives of religion to be so powerful, that, without them, it were impossible for civil society to subsist; nor are they ashamed of so palpable a contradiction. It is certain, from experience, that the smallest grain of natural honesty and benevolence has more effect on men's conduct, than the most pompous views suggested by theological theories and systems. A man's natural inclination works incessantly upon him; it is for ever present to the mind; and mingles itself with every view and consideration: Whereas religious motives, where they act at all, operate only by starts and bounds; and it is scarcely possible for them to become altogether habitual to the mind. The force of the greatest gravity, say the philosophers, is infinitely small, in comparison of that of the least impulse; yet it is certain that the smallest gravity will, in the end, prevail above a great impulse; because no strokes or blows can be repeated with such constancy as attraction and gravitation.

Another advantage of inclination: It engages on its side all the wit and ingenuity of the mind; and when set in opposition to religious principles, seeks every method and art of eluding them: In which it is almost always successful. Who can explain the heart of man, or account for those strange salvos and excuses, with which people satisfy themselves, when they follow their inclinations, in opposition to their religious duty? This is well understood in the world; and none but fools ever repose less trust in a man, because they hear, that, from study and philosophy, he has entertained some speculative doubts with regard to theological subjects. And when we have to do with a man, who makes a great profession of religion and devotion; has this any other effect upon several, who pass for prudent, than to put them on their guard, lest they be cheated and deceived by him?

We must farther consider, that philosophers, who cultivate reason and reflection, stand less in need of such motives to keep them under the restraint of morals: And that the vulgar, who alone may need them, are utterly incapable of so pure a religion as represents the Deity to be pleased with nothing but virtue in human behaviour.

The recommendations to the Divinity are generally supposed to be either frivolous observances, or rapturous ecstasies, or a bigoted credulity. We need not run back into antiquity, or wander into remote regions, to find instances of this degeneracy. Amongst ourselves, some have been guilty of that atrociousness, unknown to the EGYPTIAN and GRECIAN superstitions, of declaiming, in express terms, against morality, and representing it as a sure forfeiture of the divine favour, if the least trust or reliance be laid upon it.

But even though superstition or enthusiasm should not put itself in direct opposition to morality; the very diverting of the attention, the raising up a new and frivolous species of merit, the preposterous distribution which it makes of praise and blame, must have the most pernicious consequences, and weaken extremely men's attachment to the natural motives of justice and humanity.

Such a principle of action likewise, not being any of the familiar motives of human conduct, acts only by intervals on the temper, and must be roused by continual efforts, in order to render the pious zealot satisfied with his own conduct, and make him fulfil his devotional task. Many religious exercises are entered into with seeming fervour, where the heart, at the time, feels cold and languid: A habit of dissimulation is by degrees contracted: And fraud and falsehood become the predominant principle. Hence the reason of that vulgar observation, that the highest zeal in religion and the deepest hypocrisy, so far from being inconsistent, are often or commonly united in the same individual character.

The bad effects of such habits, even in common life, are easily imagined: But where the interests of religion are concerned, no morality can be forcible enough to bind the enthusiastic zealot. The sacredness of the cause sanctifies every measure which can be made use of to promote it.

The steady attention alone to so important an interest as that of eternal salvation is apt to extinguish the benevolent affections, and beget a narrow, contracted selfishness. And when such a temper is encouraged, it easily eludes all the general precepts of charity and benevolence.

Thus the motives of vulgar superstition have no great influence on general conduct; nor is their operation very favourable to morality, in the instances where they predominate.

Is there any maxim in politics more certain and infallible, than that both the number and authority of priests should be confined within very narrow limits, and that the civil magistrate ought, for ever, to keep his *fasces* and *axes* from such dangerous hands? But if the spirit of popular religion were so salutary to society, a contrary maxim ought to prevail. The greater number of priests, and their greater authority and riches, will always augment the religious spirit. And though the priests have the guidance of this spirit, why may we not expect a superior sanctity of life, and greater benevolence and moderation, from persons who are set apart for religion, who are continually inculcating it upon others, and who must themselves imbibe a greater share of it? Whence comes it then, that, in fact, the utmost a wise magistrate can propose with regard to popular religions, is, as far as possible, to make a saving game of it, and to prevent their pernicious consequences with regard to society? Every expedient which he tries for so humble a purpose is surrounded with inconveniences. If he admits only one religion among his subjects, he must sacrifice, to an uncertain prospect of tranquillity, every consideration of public liberty, science, reason, industry, and even his own independency. If he gives indulgence to several sects, which is the wiser maxim, he must preserve a very philosophical indifference to all of them, and carefully restrain the pretensions of the prevailing sect; otherwise he can expect nothing but endless disputes, quarrels, factions, persecutions, and civil commotions.

True religion, I allow, has no such pernicious consequences: But we must treat of religion, as it has commonly been found in the world; nor have I any thing to do with that speculative tenet of theism, which, as it is a species of philosophy, must partake of the beneficial influence of that principle, and at the same time must lie under a like inconvenience, of being always confined to very few persons.

Oaths are requisite in all courts of judicature; but it is a question whether their authority arises from any popular religion. It is the solemnity and importance of the occasion, the regard to reputation, and the reflecting on the general interests of society, which are the chief restraints upon mankind. Custom-house oaths and political oaths are but little regarded even by some who pretend to principles of honesty and religion: And a Quaker's asseveration is with us justly put upon the same footing with the oath of any other person. I know, that POLYBIUS ascribes the infamy of GREEK faith to the prevalency of the EPICUREAN philosophy; but I know also, that PUNIC faith had as bad a reputation in ancient times, as IRISH evidence has in modern; though we cannot account for these vulgar observations by the same reason. Not to mention, that GREEK faith was infamous before the rise of the EPICUREAN philosophy; and EURIPIDES, in a passage which I shall point out to you, has glanced a remarkable

stroke of satire against his nation, with regard to this circumstance.

Take care, PHILO, replied CLEANTHES, take care: Push
not matters too far: Allow not your zeal against false religion to undermine your veneration for the true. Forfeit
not this principle, the chief, the only great comfort in life;
and our principle support amidst all the attacks of
adverse fortune. The most agreeable reflection, which it
is possible for human imagination to suggest, is that of
genuine theism, which represents us as the workmanship
of a Being perfectly good, wise, and powerful; who cre-
ated us for happiness, and who, having implanted in us
immeasurable desires of good, will prolong our existence
to all eternity, and will transfer us into an infinite variety
of scenes, in order to satisfy those desires, and render
our felicity complete and durable. Next to such a Being
himself (if the comparison be allowed) the happiest lot
which we can imagine, is that of being under his
guardianship and protection.

These appearances, said PHILO, are most engaging
and alluring; and with regard to the true philosopher,
they are more than appearances. But it happens here, as
in the former case, that, with regard to the greater part of
mankind, the appearances are deceitful, and that the terrors of religion commonly prevail above its comforts.

It is allowed, that men never have recourse to devotion so readily as when dejected with grief or depressed
with sickness. Is not this a proof, that the religious spirit
is not so nearly allied to joy as to sorrow?

But men, when afflicted, find consolation in religion,
replied CLEANTHES. Sometimes, said PHILO: But it is natural
to imagine, that they will form a notion of those
unknown Beings, suitably to the present gloom and
melancholy of their temper, when they betake themselves

to the contemplation of them. Accordingly, we find the tremendous images to predominate in all religions; and we ourselves, after having employed the most exalted expression in our descriptions of the Deity, fall into the flattest contradiction, in affirming, that the damned are infinitely superior in number to the elect.

I shall venture to affirm, that there never was a popular religion, which represented the state of departed souls in such a light, as would render it eligible for human kind, that there should be such a state. These fine models of religion are the mere product of philosophy. For as death lies between the eye and the prospect of futurity, that event is so shocking to nature, that it must throw a gloom on all the regions which lie beyond it; and suggest to the generality of mankind the idea of CERBERUS and FURIES; devils, and torrents of fire and brimstone.

It is true; both fear and hope enter into religion; because both these passions, at different times, agitate the human mind, and each of them forms a species of divinity, suitable to itself. But when a man is in a cheerful disposition, he is fit for business or company or entertainment of any kind; and he naturally applies himself to these, and thinks not of religion. When melancholy, and dejected, he has nothing to do but brood upon the terrors of the invisible world, and to plunge himself still deeper in affliction. It may, indeed, happen, that after he has, in this manner, engraved the religious opinions deep into his thought and imagination, there may arrive a change of health or circumstances, which may restore his good humour, and raising cheerful prospects of futurity, make him run into the other extreme of joy and triumph. But still it must be acknowledged, that, as terror is the primary principle of religion, it is the passion which always predominates in it, and admits but of short intervals of pleasure.

Not to mention, that these fits of excessive, enthusiastic joy, by exhausting the spirits, always prepare the way for equal fits of superstitious terror and dejection; nor is there any state of mind so happy as the calm and equable. But this state it is impossible to support, where a man thinks, that he lies, in such profound darkness and uncertainty, between an eternity of happiness and an eternity of misery. No wonder, that such an opinion disjoints the ordinary frame of the mind, and throws it into the utmost confusion. And though that opinion is seldom so steady in its operation as to influence all the actions; yet it is apt to make a considerable breach in the temper, and to produce that gloom and melancholy, so remarkable in all devout people.

It is contrary to common sense to entertain apprehensions or terrors, upon account of any opinion whatsoever, or to imagine that we run any risk hereafter, by the freest use of our reason. Such a sentiment implies both an *absurdity* and an *inconsistency*. It is an absurdity to believe that the Deity has human passions, and one of the lowest of human passions, a restless appetite for applause. It is an inconsistency to believe, that, since the Deity has this human passion, he has not others also; and, in particular, a disregard to the opinions of creatures so much inferior.

[*To know God*, says Seneca, *is to worship him*. All other worship is indeed absurd, superstitious, and even impious. It degrades him to the low condition of mankind, who are delighted with entreaty, solicitation, presents, and flattery. Yet is this impiety the smallest of which superstition is guilty. Commonly, it depresses the Deity far below the condition of mankind; and represents him as a capricious Dæmon, who exercises his power without reason and without humanity! And were that divine Being disposed to be offended at the vices and follies of silly mortals, who are his own workmanship; ill would it surely fare with the votaries of most popular superstitions. Nor would any of human race merit his *favour*, but a very few, the philosophical theists, who entertain, or rather indeed endeavour to entertain, suitable notions of his divine perfections: As the only persons entitled to his *compassion* and *indulgence* would be the philosophical sceptics, a sect almost equally rare, who, from a natural diffidence of their own capacity, suspend, or endeavour to suspend all judgment with regard to such sublime and such extraordinary subjects.]

If the whole of natural theology, as some people seem to maintain, resolves itself into one simple, though somewhat ambiguous, at least undefined proposition, *that the cause or causes of order in the universe probably bear some remote analogy to human intelligence:* If this proposition be not capable of extension, variation, or more particular explication: If it afford no inference that affects human life, or can be the source of any action or forbearance: And if the analogy, imperfect as it is, can be carried no farther than to the human intelligence; and cannot be transferred, with any appearance of probability, to the other qualities of the mind: If this really be the case, what can the most inquisitive, contemplative, and religious man do more than give a plain, philosophical assent to the proposition, as often as it occurs; and believe that the arguments, on which it is established, exceed the objections which lie against it? Some astonishment indeed will naturally arise from the greatness of the object: Some melancholy from its obscurity: Some contempt of human reason, that it can give no solution more satisfactory with regard to so extraordinary and magnificent a question. But believe me, CLEANTHES, the most natural sentiment, which a well-disposed mind will feel on this occasion, is a longing desire and expectation, that Heaven would be pleased to dissipate, at least alleviate, this profound ignorance, by affording some more particular revelation to mankind, and making discoveries of the nature, attributes, and operations of the divine object of our Faith. A person, seasoned with a just sense of the imperfections of natural reason, will fly to revealed truth with the greatest avidity: While the haughty dogmatist, persuaded that he can erect a complete system of theology by the mere help of philosophy, disdains any farther aid, and rejects this adventitious instructor. To be a philosophical sceptic is, in a man of letters, the first and most essential step towards being a sound, believing Christian; a proposition which I would willingly recommend to the attention of PAMPHILUS: And I hope CLEANTHES will forgive me for interposing so far in the education and instruction of his pupil.

CLEANTHES and PHILO pursued not this conversation much farther; and as nothing ever made greater impression on me, than all the reasonings of that day; so I confess, that, upon a serious review of the whole, I cannot but think, that PHILO's principles are more probable than DEMEA's; but that those of CLEANTHES approach still nearer to the truth.

Index